Great Sentences for Great Paragraphs

D1295449

Great Sentences for Great Paragraphs

An Introduction to Basic Sentences and Paragraphs

Keith S. Folse, Ph.D.
Coordinator, M.A. TESOL Program,
University of Central Florida

April Muchmore-Vokoun
English Language Institute,
University of South Florida

Elena Vestri Solomon
Senior English Language Fellow,
Uzbekistan Teachers of English Association

Houghton Mifflin Company
Boston   New York

Editor in Chief: Patricia A. Coryell
Director of ESL Publishing: Susan Maguire
Senior Development Editor: Kathy Sands Boehmer
Editorial Assistant: Mira Bharin
Senior Project Editor: Kathryn Dinovo
Senior Manufacturing Coordinator: Jane Spelman
Marketing Manager: Annamarie Rice
Marketing Associate: Claudia Martínez

Cover Image: Harold Burch

college.hmco.com

Printed in the U.S.A.

Library of Congress Control Number: 2001131494

ISBN: 0-618-05617-3

123456789-CRS-05 04 03 02 01

Contents

Part II   Developing Sentences   58

Overview

Great Sentences for Great Paragraphs is the lower-level book of the *Great Paragraphs* and *Great Essays* series of composition books. In *Great Sentences*, students become better writers by focusing their attention on the elements of writing a good sentence within simple paragraphs. This book provides practice that helps students not only to understand the writing process but also to produce a correct final written product.

The book is designed for students who are novice writers. It is especially suited for beginning to lower intermediate students but may be used with any level writer who is unfamiliar with the basics of writing correct sentences in simple paragraphs. Depending on the class level and the amount of writing that is done outside of class, there is enough material for 60 to 80 classroom hours. If more of the writing is done outside of class, the number of hours for a faster group can be as few as 40.

Great Sentences contains 147 activities with at least 70 suggestions for additional writing. In addition, the appendices contain supplementary instruction and practices in a wide variety of writing components, including capitalization, spelling rules, articles, prepositions, commas, and adjectives. Of special interest to teachers is Appendix 14, which contains extra writing activities for students who need additional help or practice.

A very important feature of *Great Sentences* is the inclusion of 70 sample paragraphs distributed throughout the activities. Instead of exercises consisting of unrelated sentences, most of the activities in this book present whole paragraphs of related sentences on a single topic. In addition to providing relevant practice on some aspect of the sentence, these contextualized activities also provide learners with more input in English composition and in paragraph organization and cohesion.

For many ESL students, not being able to write effectively and easily in English is a major obstacle to their future educational plans. Thus, the quality of any written work is important. To this end, the activities in this book deal with different elements that can affect the quality of a written product, including grammar, punctuation, and capitalization.

Some ESL students are already good writers in their native language, but others need work in the basic steps involved in the process of composing sentences and paragraphs. These students in particular will benefit from the step-by-step activities in *Great Sentences*.

The teacher is always the best judge of which units and which activities should be covered with any group of students. It is up to you to gauge the needs of your students and then match those needs with the material in this book.

TEXT ORGANIZATION

UNITS 1–8

Great Sentences consists of eight units. Unit 1 and Units 3 through 7 deal with a particular aspect of writing correct sentences in simple paragraphs. Unit 2 introduces students to the basic elements of a paragraph and asks students to analyze these elements. Unit 8 contains an additional 24 writing activities.

In Unit 1, students learn the basic parts of a sentence. Students learn the importance of subjects and verbs in a sentence.

In Unit 2, students see the connection between sentences and paragraphs. Novice writers learn the basic parts of a paragraph and how their sentences can fit into these parts.

In Unit 3, students write about the present. This unit practices writing with simple present tense.

In Unit 4, students write about the past. Here students practice simple past tense of both regular and irregular verbs.

In Unit 5, students practice describing actions. The writing activities in this unit guide students through the use of the present progressive (continuous) tense to accomplish this.

In Unit 6, students write about the future. They have numerous opportunities to use *be + going to* in their writing and to compare this to the tenses that they have learned in previous units of this book.

Unit 7 offers a more difficult but necessary lesson in writing. Here students learn to build better sentences by using adjective clauses in their writing. Students learn not only the structure of these clauses but also correct placement and punctuation within sentences.

Unit 8 consists of 24 activities that provide further guided and free practice of the techniques presented in this text. These activities may be done toward the end of the course, or they may be done while the students are still working in the first seven units of the book. In addition, these activities may be used as remedial help for weaker students or for bonus work for students who have already finished the work in the first seven units.

APPENDICES

Great Sentences contains 16 appendices. Appendices 1 through 13 offer instruction in a wide array of basic writing areas, including capitalization, spelling rules for adding *-ed*, irregular past tense, spelling rules for adding *-ing*, stative verbs, definite article *the*, non-count nouns, possessive adjectives, quantifiers, prepositions, comma rules, order of adjectives, and definitions of useful language terms. The material is presented in a very simple yet clear manner and is accompanied by pertinent examples.

Appendix 14 is a collection of ten guided paragraph activities. Many of these activities require students to read and study short paragraphs, make a series of basic changes, and then rewrite their new paragraph. Other activities are more open-ended. These activities are designed to be done as additional work to support or supplement the material within the main units of the book.

Appendix 15 consists of the peer editing sheets for the peer editing activity in each unit. While we believe that the best way to learn to edit is to practice editing, we believe that lower-level students in particular should not edit written work without the kind of guidance (i.e., teaching) that is provided by these peer editing sheets.

Appendix 16 is the Answer Key.

CONTENTS OF A UNIT

Though each unit has a specific writing goal and Grammar and Sentence Structure, the following features appear in almost every unit.

GRAMMAR AND SENTENCE STRUCTURE

The number one problem for many beginning (and even advanced) writers is grammar. While nonnative speakers will always make some errors, it is important to help students realize what their major grammar and sentence structure problems are and then to provide appropriate instruction and practice exercises and activities.

The grammar and sentence structure points are always language structures that are necessary to complete the writing tasks within that unit. For example, in Unit 5, Describing Actions, students are asked to pay particular attention to the use of verbs in the present progressive (continuous) tense because this language structure is necessary to write descriptions of actions. Likewise, in Unit 7, students are taught to build up sentence variety through the use of adjective clauses. Students first study about adjective clauses but are then asked to produce sentences and then small paragraphs that incorporate this sentence structure.

SENTENCE DEVELOPMENT

One of the main goals of *Great Sentences* is for students to learn the basics of the simple sentence in English. However, an equally important and related goal is for students to move beyond the simple sentence and begin including compound and complex sentences in their original writing. Thus, this section provides important practice in helping students expand their repertoire of sentence structures in English.

WRITER'S NOTES

Rather than large boxed areas overflowing with information, *Great Sentences* features small chunks of writing advice under this heading. The content of these writer's notes varies from brainstorming techniques, to peer editing guidelines, to journal writing advice, to using commas correctly.

EDITING

Teaching students to edit their own writing is one of the most important goals of any writing course. To this end, *Great Sentences* provides several kinds of editing practice and activities throughout the units.

GUIDED WRITING PRACTICE

Because of the lower proficiency of students using this book, guided writing practice activities are included. In the more basic exercises, students are asked to copy a paragraph and make only four or five rather simple changes. Eventually, the changes become more complicated. While the students are not writing original work here, they are gaining critical confidence with the conventions of good writing, such as the use of capital letters, indenting, handwriting (or typing), and punctuation.

PEER EDITING

Each unit contains an activity in which students swap papers with another student and then make comments about their partner's papers. Because of the lower proficiency level of the students, it is especially important to provide novice writers and therefore novice editors with detailed guidelines about what to look for when editing or reviewing someone's work. In addition, there is a section in Unit 1 that explains what to keep in mind when reviewing someone else's work.

JOURNAL WRITING

The best way to learn to write is by writing. Journal writing offers a happy compromise between informal letter (or e-mail) writing to friends and formal paragraph or essay writing. Journal writing encourages students to write about topics that they are interested in. To this end, each unit has a list of ten possible journal topics with a series of small questions to encourage original student writing. These topics may be developed into class assignments, but since students' purposes for learning to write in English can vary so much, we leave the topics and parameters for course writing up to the individual instructor.

ABOUT THE ACTIVITIES AND PRACTICES

Teachers have long noticed that although students do well with grammar in discrete sentences, they may have problems with the same grammar when it occurs in a paragraph. Because of this, most of the activities and practices in *Great Sentences* work with complete paragraphs. Thus, instead of five unrelated sentences for practice with the past tense, we offer a paragraph of five sentences. Our hope is that by practicing the grammatical structure within the target medium, students will produce more accurate writing sooner. The large number of such paragraphs (70) allows a great deal of freedom on the teacher's part in planning this course.

The earliest ESL composition textbooks were merely extensions of ESL grammar classes. The activities in these books did not practice English composition as much as they did ESL grammar points. Later books, on the other hand, tended to focus too much on the composing process. We feel that this focus ignores the important fact that the real goal for our ESL students is both to produce a presentable product and to understand the composing practice. From our years of ESL and other L2 teaching experience, we believe that *Great Sentences* allows students to achieve this goal.

ACKNOWLEDGMENTS

We would like to thank ESL and English composition colleagues who generously shared their ideas, insights, and feedback on L2 writing, community college and university English course requirements, and textbook design. In addition, we would like to thank teachers on two electronic lists, TESL-L and TESLIE-L, who responded to our original queries and thereby helped us write this book.

We offer special thanks to our incredible editors at Houghton Mifflin. Susan Maguire has been a constant source of guidance and inspiration throughout the completion of not only *Great Sentences* but also *Great Paragraphs* and *Great Essays*. Likewise, we are indebted to Kathy Sands Boehmer, who offered us ideas and feedback and helped us keep ourselves and this writing project on schedule. In addition, we are indebted to our development editor, Kathleen Smith, whose careful editing and diligent work have played a major part in this final product.

We would also like to thank the following reviewers who offered ideas and suggestions that shaped our revisions:

Richard Cervin, Sacramento City College, CA

Eileen Cotter, Montgomery College, MD

Marjorie Wilma Parker, Northern Virginia Community College, VA

Dianne Ruggiero, Broward Community College

Susan Stann, DeAnza College, CA

Finally, many thanks go to our students, who have taught us what composition ought to be, and to the numerous teachers who have given us such positive feedback on our earlier works, *Great Paragraphs* and *Great Essays*. Without these people, this work would most certainly have been impossible.

Keith S. Folse
April Muchmore-Vokoun
Elena Vestri Solomon

Great Sentences for Great Paragraphs

Part I

The English Sentence

Unit 2   Connecting Sentences and Paragraphs

Unit 1

Understanding Sentence Basics

GOAL: To learn how to write a correct simple sentence

SENTENCE DEVELOPMENT: Simple sentences

GRAMMAR AND SENTENCE STRUCTURE: Subjects and verbs

WHAT IS A SENTENCE?

A sentence is a group of words that expresses a complete thought. The words in a sentence are in a special order. Sentences are made of words. In order to know what a sentence is, you need to start with words.

WORDS

A word represents an idea. It is made from one or more letters. Examples of words are *pencil*, *tree*, *spaghetti*, *run*, and *slow*.

Do You Know?

The words on the left are English. The words on the right are not English. Do you know what language they are? Try to guess the languages, and then check your answers on page 237.

English	Not English	English	Not English
cat	gato	cold	samui
please	te rog	delicious	sedap
thanks	shukran	window	chang-moon
fall	tomber		

SENTENCES

A sentence is a group of words that expresses a complete thought. Examples of sentences are *Joe likes basketball.* and *The weather is cold today.*

Do You Know?

The sentences on the left are English. The sentences on the right are not English. Do you know what language they are? Try to guess the languages, and then check your answers on page 237.

The class has twelve students.	Ci sono dodici studenti nella classe.
Canada is in North America.	這位學生是來自加拿大。
Mike speaks French and English.	Miklós beszél franciául és angolul.
A cat has a tail and four legs.	Pisica are o coadă și patru picioare.

Words, sentences, paragraphs, and essays are all related. Words can go together to make sentences. Sentences can go together to make a paragraph. Finally, paragraphs can be combined into an essay. In this book, you will study sentences. Then you will study sentences in paragraphs.

Connections

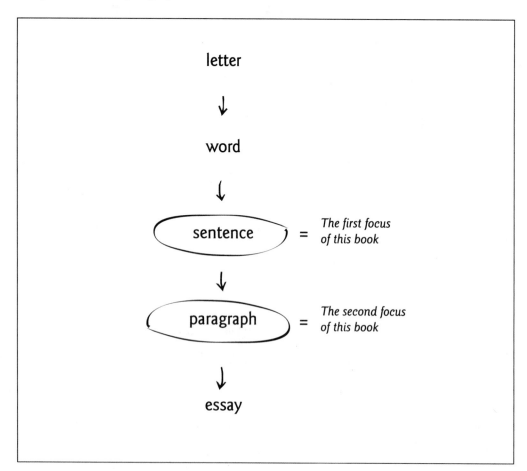

letter

↓

word

↓

(sentence)   =   *The first focus of this book*

↓

(paragraph)   =   *The second focus of this book*

↓

essay

Activity 1 — Words into Sentences

The sentences below are not correct. The words are in the wrong order. Write the words in the correct order to make correct English sentences. The first one has been done for you.

Topic: Write about your family.

1. is not / very big / My family / .   My family is not very big. _____

2. only four people / There are / .   _____

3. I / two parents / have / .   _____

4. José / my father's name / is / .   _____

5. My mother's name / is / Karina / .   _____

6. have / I / one brother / .   _____

7. His name / Andy / is / .   _____

8. very much / I / my family / love / .   _____

Activity 2 — Writing Simple Sentences: A Diagnostic

Write five to eight sentences about your family. Follow the examples in Activity 1.

Topic: Write about your family.

1. _____

2. _____

3. _____

4. _____

5. _____

6. _____

7. _____

8. _____

WORKING WITH SENTENCES

In this section you will learn the basics of how to write simple sentences, including capitalization and some punctuation rules.

WRITER'S NOTE: Begin a Sentence with a Capital Letter

In English, there are two kinds of letters: capital letters (H, R) and small letters (h, r). Most of the time we use small letters. However, we always begin a sentence with a capital letter.

Incorrect:	the boxes on the table are heavy.
Correct:	**The** boxes on the table are heavy.
Incorrect:	where do you live?
Correct:	**Where** do you live?

Look back at every sentence in the unit so far. Can you find any sentences that do not begin with a capital letter? (The answer is "no"!)

(NOTE: See Appendix 1 for capitalization rules.)

In English, there are three ways to end a sentence:

- with a period (.)
- with a question mark (?)
- with an exclamation point (!)

WRITER'S NOTE: End a Sentence with a Period

The most common or usual way to end a sentence is with a period.

A sentence that tells us information is called a statement. We usually put a period at the end of a sentence that is a statement. For example, this sentence has a period at the end. Can you find any sentences in this unit that do not end with a period? (The answer is "yes"!)

Incorrect:	Brazil is a large country
Correct:	Brazil is a large country**.**
Incorrect:	I don't like coffee with sugar
Correct:	I don't like coffee with sugar**.**

Activity 3	Unscrambling and Writing Sentences

Unscramble the groups of words below to write simple sentences. Be sure to begin each sentence with a capital letter. In addition, be sure to put a period at the end of sentences that tell you information.

Topic: Write about something good to eat.

1. spaghetti / most kids / like

   _____

2. enjoy / they / the taste of spaghetti

   _____

3. the smell of spaghetti / they / love

   _____

4. tomato sauce / on their spaghetti / some kids / put

   _____

5. like / on their spaghetti / cheese / other kids

   _____

Activity 4   **Writing Simple Sentences**

Copy the sentences you unscrambled in Activity 3. In every sentence, change the word spaghetti *to some other food that kids like. Make other appropriate changes as necessary.*

1. _____

2. _____

3. _____

4. _____

5. _____

Editing

Activity 5   **Editing Simple Sentences**

Read this list of ten sentences about a taxi driver. In each sentence, correct the capitalization mistakes and add a period at the end. Then write the sentences on another piece of paper. The first one has been done for you.

LIGHTNING
TAXI SERVICE

Topic: Write about a person and his or her job.

1. ~~t~~his is my cousin. ^T

2. his name is Albert

3. albert is a taxi driver

4. he is a good taxi driver

5. albert works for a large taxi company

6. the name of the taxi company is Lightning Taxi Service

7. albert drives a taxi six days a week

8. he meets interesting people from many different places

WRITER'S NOTE: Using Capital Letters

Proper Nouns

In English, the name of a specific person, place, or thing always begins with a capital letter. These types of words are called proper nouns. *George Washington* is the name of a specific person. *San Francisco* is the name of a specific place. *Pepsi* is the name of a specific thing. Can you think of more examples?

Incorrect:	My friend john works in chicago.
Correct:	My friend John works in Chicago. (*a specific person, a specific place*)
Incorrect:	lucille and robby drink coca-cola.
Correct:	Lucille and Robby drink Coca-Cola. (*specific people, a specific thing*)

Common Nouns

Common nouns do not begin with a capital letter. They begin with a small letter. Some examples of common nouns are *car, computer, garage, snow, television.*

More Capital Letters

In English, many other kinds of words begin with capital letters. Here are some examples.

Days of the week

Incorrect:	My birthday is on monday.
Correct:	My birthday is on Monday.

Months

Incorrect:	The shortest month of the year is february.
Correct:	The shortest month of the year is February.

Languages

Incorrect:	Sireesha speaks hindi.
Correct:	Sireesha speaks Hindi.

Countries

Incorrect:	My father is from thailand.
Correct:	My father is from Thailand.

WRITER'S NOTE: Question Marks

In English, you can end a sentence with a question mark (?). *Do you understand this? Do you have any questions?* These are examples of questions. They have a question mark at the end.

Incorrect:	Is Brazil a large country.
Correct:	Is Brazil a large country?
Incorrect:	Where do you live.
Correct:	Where do you live?

Geography

Activity 6   Geography Quiz

How well do you know geography? Use the words below to write questions about geography.
Then write the answers in complete sentences. Make sure the words are in the correct order.
Be careful to use capital letters and punctuation. The first one has been done for you.

1. what / the capital / of brazil / is

   Question: _What is the capital of Brazil?_____

   Answer: _The capital of Brazil is Brasilia._____

2. is / what city / the white house in

   Question: _____

   Answer: _____

3. what country / the nile river in / is

   Question: _____

   Answer: _____

4. what city / is / the eiffel tower in

   Question: _____

   Answer: _____

5. what / the biggest city / in mexico / is

   Question: _____

   Answer: _____

6. where / are / the andes mountains

   Question: _____

   Answer: _____

7. is / what / the capital of saudi arabia

   Question: _____

   Answer: _____

8. what / the biggest province / is / in canada

Question: _____

Answer: _____

WRITER'S NOTE: Exclamation Points

You use an exclamation point (!) to show emphasis or emotion about something. Exclamation points are not used often, but when a sentence expresses surprise, it is appropriate to use an exclamation point.

Incorrect:	It's snowing.
Correct:	It's snowing!
Incorrect:	I won the lottery last night?
Correct:	I won the lottery last night!

Activity 7   **Statement, Question, or Exclamation**

Read each sentence. If it is a statement, put S on the line and a period (.) at the end of the sentence. If it is a question, write Q on the line and put a question mark (?) at the end of the question. If it is an exclamation, write E on the line and put an exclamation point (!) at the end of the sentence. The first two have been done for you.

February

SUN	MON	TUE	WED	THU	FRI	SAT
						1
2	3	4	5	6	7	8
9	10	11	12	13	14	15
16	17	18	19	20	21	22
23	24	25	26	27	28	

1. __Q__ How many days are in a month?

2. __S__ The answer depends on the month.

3. _____ Some months have thirty days

4. _____ An example of this is September

5. _____ Other months have thirty-one days

6. _____ Examples are July and December

7. _____ What month never has thirty days

8. _____ The answer is February

9. _____ February usually has twenty-eight days

10. _____ Everyone in my family was born in February

Activity 8   **Interview: Writing Information**

Copy the questions on the lines. Be sure to use capital letters and question marks. Ask a class-mate the questions. Then write your classmate's answers. Use capital letters and periods.

1. what is your name

   Question: _____

   Answer: _____

2. where are you from

   Question: _____

   Answer: _____

3. where do you live

   Question: _____

   Answer: _____

4. how many people are in your family

Question: _____

Answer: _____

5. do you have a car

Question: _____

Answer: _____

6. what food do you like to eat

Question: _____

Answer: _____

7. what is your favorite place to visit

Question: _____

Answer: _____

8. what is your favorite movie

Question: _____

Answer: _____

Editing

Activity 9   **Editing Scrambled Sentences**

Here are some sentences about Costa Rica. The words and phrases in each sentence are scrambled. First, put the sentence parts in the correct order. Then add capital letters. Add a period, a question mark, or an exclamation point.

Topic: Write about a country.

1. costa rica / where / is

_____

2. in central america / a country / costa rica / is

_____

3. between panama and nicaragua / it / is

_____

4. it / is / between the atlantic ocean and the pacific ocean

_____

5. approximately two million / is / the population

_____

6. many tourists / there / go

_____

7. wild animals / they / see / in the jungle

_____

8. in the world / the most beautiful country / it is

_____

9. want to visit / I / this beautiful country

_____

10. costa rica / do you want to visit

_____

Activity 10	Guided Writing Practice

Answer the following questions and write eight to ten sentences about a country. Write capital letters, periods, question marks, and exclamation points correctly.

Topic: Write about a country.

1. What country do you want to visit? _____

2. Why do you want to visit this country? _____

   _____

   _____

3. Where is this country located? _____

   _____

4. How big is this country? _____

   _____

5. What is the capital of this country? _____

   _____

6. What is one famous monument or important location in this country? _____

   _____

7. Briefly describe this monument or location. _____

   _____

   _____

8. What do you know about the food in this country? _____

   _____

   _____

THE PARTS OF A SENTENCE: SUBJECT AND VERB

Every English sentence must have a subject and a verb.

The Simple Sentence

The basic sentence pattern that you are studying in this unit is called a **simple sentence**. A simple sentence has one subject and one verb.

subject   ➜   **verb**

Maria   plays the harp.

GRAMMAR AND SENTENCE STRUCTURE: Subjects and Verbs

In English, every sentence has two main parts: the subject and the verb. As you study the following simple sentences, look for this pattern.

Subject

The subject is the person or thing that does the action. The subject comes before the verb. Look at these simple sentences. The subjects are underlined.

That little boy swims every day.

People in China speak Chinese.

Seven is my lucky number.

Verb

The verb is usually the action word in the sentence. The verb comes after the subject. Examples of verbs are *go*, *speak*, *write*, *swim*, and *watch*. Some verbs do not have much action. Examples are *be (am, is, are, was, were)*, *like*, *want*, and *need*. Look at these simple sentences. The verbs are circled.

That little boy (swims) every day.

People in China (speak) Chinese.

Seven (is) my lucky number.

Checking for the Subject and the Verb

Every sentence should have a subject and a verb. It is easy for student writers to leave out the subject or the verb. A sentence without a subject or without a verb is called a fragment. A fragment is a piece of a sentence.

Incorrect:	John is my brother. Works at Ames Bank in Miami. (*no subject*)
Correct:	John is my brother. He works at Ames Bank in Miami.
Incorrect:	Most Japanese people a white car. (*no verb*)
Correct:	Most Japanese people have a white car.
Correct:	Most Japanese people drive a white car.

When you write, check to make sure each sentence has a subject for the verb and a verb for the subject.

Commands

In command (imperative) sentences, the subject is *you.* However, the word *you* is not usually stated.

Examples: Open the door now! (NOT: *You* open the door now!)

Don't say that word. (NOT: *You* don't say that word.)

Activity 11	**Sentence or Fragment**

Read each group of words. If it is a fragment, write F on the line. If it is a complete sentence, write S on the line. The first two have been done for you.

1. ____S____ Billy Mitchell lives in a big apartment.

2. ____F____ My mother breakfast every morning.

3. _____ Is incredibly delicious.

4. _____ Does Carol have a car?

5. _____ They my cousins from Miami.

6. _____ You a student?

7. _____ Michael likes classical music.

8. _____ Nancy and Jeanine very best friends.

9. _____ The girls play soccer after school.

10. _____ I am from Colombia.

Activity 12	**Subjects**

Read each sentence. Underline the subject.

1. Tuna salad is easy to make.

2. The ingredients are simple and cheap.

3. Two ingredients are tuna fish and mayonnaise.

4. I also use onions, salt, and pepper.

5. First, I cut up the onions.

6. Then I add the tuna fish and the mayonnaise.

7. Finally, I add some salt and a lot of pepper.

8. Tuna salad is my favorite food!

Activity 13   **Subjects and Verbs**

Read the simple sentences in this paragraph. Underline each subject. Circle each verb. The first one has been done for you.

Paragraph 1

EXAMPLE PARAGRAPH

Making Tuna Salad

<u>Tuna salad</u> (is) easy to make. The ingredients are simple and cheap. Two ingredients are tuna fish and mayonnaise. I also use onions, salt, and pepper. First, I cut up the onions. Then I add the tuna fish and the mayonnaise. Finally, I add some salt and a lot of pepper. Tuna salad is my favorite food!

SENTENCES IN PARAGRAPHS

You can put sentences together to make a paragraph. All the sentences in a paragraph are about the same topic.

WRITER'S NOTE: Sentences and Paragraphs

A group of words that tell about one idea is called a sentence. A group of sentences that tell about one topic or one idea is called a paragraph.

Look at the sentences in Activity 12 and Activity 13 again. How are they different? In Activity 12, eight sentences are in a list. In Activity 13, the same eight sentences are not in a list. They are in a special format. This format is called a paragraph. What do you know about paragraphs? You will study much more about paragraphs beginning in Unit 2.

| Activity 14 | Word Order of Subjects and Verbs |

Underline the correct subject and verb in parentheses ( ). Remember to put the subject before the verb.

Paragraph 2

EXAMPLE PARAGRAPH

A Great Place to Work

(**1.** Caroline Jimenez works / Works Caroline Jimenez) at Anderson Supermarket. (**2.** Works she / She works) there on Mondays and Thursdays. On Wednesdays (**3.** attends she / she attends) classes at Jefferson Community College. (**4.** Caroline wakes up / Wakes up Caroline) at 6 A.M. (**5.** She starts / Starts she) work at 8 A.M. (**6.** Works she / She works) from 8 A.M. to 5 P.M. (**7.** Is her lunch break / Her lunch break is) from 12:30 to 1:30. (**8.** Caroline likes / Likes Caroline) her job. (**9.** Enjoys she / She enjoys) meeting people. (**10.** She loves / Loves she) her co-workers. For Caroline, (**11.** is Anderson Supermarket / Anderson Supermarket is) a great place to work.

WRITER'S NOTE: The Title of a Paragraph

What is the title of this book? Look on the front cover. Write the title here:

_____

What is the title of the paragraph in Activity 13? Write the title here:

_____

A title tells you what you will find in a book, a movie, a story, or a paragraph. A title is not a sentence. A title is usually very short. Sometimes a title is only one word, such as the movie title *Jaws*. Can you think of other movie titles in English that are only one word long?

Look at the title of Paragraph 1 in Activity 13 (Making Tuna Salad). Now look at the title of Paragraph 2 in Activity 14 (A Great Place to Work). These are good titles because they are short. They are also good titles because they tell what the paragraph is about.

In this book, give a title to every paragraph that you write.

Editing

Activity 15   **Editing Simple Sentences**

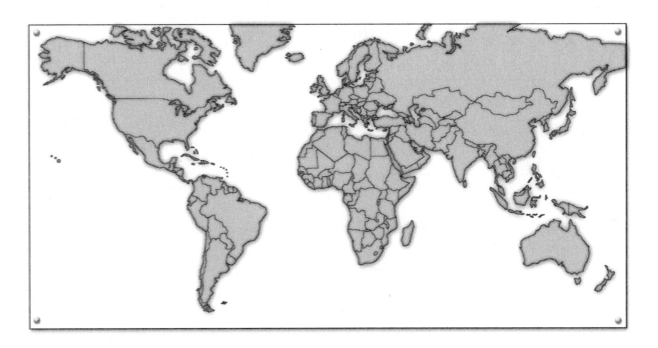

Read these ten sentences about world geography. Some of the sentences have errors with fragments (missing subject or missing verb), punctuation, or capitalization. If the sentence is correct, write C on the line. If the sentence contains an error, write X on the line and tell what the error is. Then write the correct sentence below. Follow the examples.

Examples:

X (fragment—verb missing)   Mexico not near Great Britain.

Mexico is not near Great Britain.

X (capitalization)   The Statue of Liberty is in new york.

The Statue of Liberty is in New York.

1. _____ Burundi is in africa.

_____

2. _____ Canada bigger than the United States.

_____

3. _____ A popular city in Florida is Miami?

_____

4. _____ Nepal is north of India.

_____

5. _____ Visits the Mayan ruins in Central America every year!

_____

6. _____ Bolivia no seaports.

_____

7. _____ Three main groups of people live in Malaysia.

_____

8. _____ Austria and Hungary in Europe.

_____

9. _____ Is between Mexico and Canada.

_____

10. _____ Of Thailand is about 30,000,000.

_____

Editing

Activity 16   Editing: Grammar and Sentence Review

Read the following paragraph. There are nine mistakes: four (4) missing be verbs, two (2) missing subjects, two (2) capitalization mistakes, and one (1) punctuation mistake. Find and correct the mistakes. The first one has been done for you.

Paragraph 3

The Beauty of Tuscany

Tuscany⁀ a beautiful region in Italy. Is famous for cities such as florence, Siena, and Pisa.
(is inserted above, caret below "Tuscany")

The appenine Hills in Tuscany? Tuscany also famous for wine making. For example, Chianti

and Montalcino wines very popular and tasty. Tuscany has so many interesting places to see.

Is a wonderful place to visit!

Activity 17   **Original Writing Practice**

Choose ONE of the practices below. For the practice you choose:

1. *Read the first question.*
2. *Fill in the answer. This will be the topic.*
3. *Then answer the questions about the topic. Be sure to use complete sentences with a subject and a verb.*
4. *After you write your sentences, check the spelling and grammar.*

Practice 1

Question 1a: What is your favorite food?

Answer 1a: My favorite food is _____ .

Question 1b: What country does this food come from?

Answer 1b: _____

Question 1c: What ingredients are in this food?

Answer 1c: _____

Question 1d: How do you prepare this food?

Answer 1d: _____

Question 1e: Why do you like this food?

Answer 1e: _____

Practice 2

Question 2a: What food do you like to cook?

Answer 2a: I like to cook _____ .

Question 2b: What ingredients do you need?

Answer 2b: _____

Question 2c: What is the first thing you do?

Answer 2c: _____

Question 2d: What do you do next?

Answer 2d: _____

Question 2e: How long does it take to prepare this food?

Answer 2e: _____

Practice 3

Question 3a: Who is the most interesting person in your family?

Answer 3a: The most interesting person in my family is _____ .

Question 3b: Why is this person interesting?

Answer 3b: _____

Question 3c: How old is this person?

Answer 3c: _____

Question 3d: What does this person look like?

Answer 3d: _____

Question 3e: Why do you like this person?

Answer 3e: _____

PEER EDITING

Good writers need editors to help them make their writing correct. For your writing in this book, your classmates (peers) are your editors. You will read and edit each other's paragraphs.

WRITER'S NOTE: Peer Editing for the Writer

A peer is someone who is equal to you. Your peers are the other students in your class.

It is important to hear what other people think about your writing. You need to know if they can understand your ideas. A good way to make sure that your writing is clear is to let someone else read your paper and make suggestions about it. This is called peer editing.

This is what usually happens in peer editing:

1. Another person reads your writing.

2. That person gives you suggestions and ideas for making your paper better.

3. You listen carefully to what your peer says.

4. You may want to make the changes your peer suggests. If the comments are negative, remember that the comments are about the writing, not about you!

WRITER'S NOTE: Peer Editing for the Reader

When you read your classmate's paper, be polite. Choose your words carefully. Don't say, "This is bad grammar" or "What is this?" It's better to say, "You forgot to put the word *at*" or "What does this sentence mean?"

Say things that you would like someone to tell you!

Activity 18   **Peer Editing**

*Choose someone that you work well with. Exchange papers from Activity 17. Read each other's
papers. Then use Peer Editing Sheet 1 on page 219 to help you talk about your partner's paper.*

JOURNAL WRITING

Many good writers write in a journal for practice and for ideas.

WRITER'S NOTE: Journal Writing—Write, Write, Write!

How can you become a better writer? The activities in this book will help you. The most important thing, however, is to write as much and as often as you can.

The Benefit of Practice

Think about people who can play tennis well. These people were really interested in tennis. Perhaps they read books about tennis. They probably went to see a professional tennis match. These activities alone can't make people become good tennis players. They have to practice. It doesn't matter if at first they hit the ball the wrong way. The most important thing is to hit the ball again and again. This is how people get better at tennis.

In some ways, you are like the tennis player. You want to be a good writer. Reading this book and doing the activities are helpful. Reading literature and the newspaper will help you, too. Certainly learning more grammar and vocabulary is also a good idea, but the most important thing is to write. You must write and write and write.

The best way to become a good writer in English is to write as much as possible and as often as possible.

Practice in a Journal

An excellent way to practice is to write in a journal. A journal is a notebook in which you write things every day or as often as possible. You practice expressing yourself in written English.

In a journal, you choose a specific topic and write about it. You try to express your ideas about the topic so that readers can understand what you mean. Journal topics can be general or specific. Here are some topics for journal writing:

General topics: sports, swimming, food, pets, travel, fashion, music

Specific topics: my favorite sport, why I am a vegetarian, my first airplane trip

Teacher Response

Your teacher will read your journal from time to time. Your teacher won't mark all of the grammar mistakes. A journal uses informal language. It's like a conversation between the writer and the teacher (reader). If you write about a city, don't take information from a book. Instead, write about why you want to visit that city or about the first time you visited it.

Your teacher may write some comments in your journal. Your teacher might make one or two comments about the language, especially if you make the same mistake over and over.

If you have any questions, you can ask your teacher in the journal. For example, if you want to know if you used a grammar point or a vocabulary word correctly, you can write a question in your journal.

SAMPLE JOURNAL

March 21

    Sometimes I feel lonely here. My parents are far away, but my brother is here. His name is Nelson. He is two years older than I am. He wants to study business administration. He looks like my father. He is 22 years old.

    Before we came here, Nelson and I went to New York City. We visited some cousins there. Hotels in New York expensive. We stayed with our cousins. That saved us a lot of money.

    I don't my cousins very often, so I was happy. Sometimes I feel bad because I don't know them very well.

    This is interesting information. I didn't know that your brother is at this school, too. Do you live together? I've been to New York City, too, and I know that hotels are VERY expensive there.

    Grammar: I circled two places where you forgot to put a verb. Can you think of some verbs for those sentences?

    It was easy to understand the message of your writing here. Keep up the good work!

Activity 19   **Journal Writing**

Here are ten ideas for journal writing. Write about as many as you can. Follow your teacher's directions. (We recommend that you skip a line after each line that you write. This gives your teacher a place to write comments.)

1. Write about your favorite pet. Why do you like this animal? Do you have one at home? What does the animal look like? What is its name? How old is it?

2. Write about your favorite type of weather. Why do you like this weather? What kinds of activities do you do in this weather?

3. Write about your mother or your father. Include their name, age, and occupation. What kind of personality does your mother or father have?

4. Write about a toy you remember from your childhood. What kind of toy was it? How long did you have it? Who gave it to you? Do you still have it? If not, what happened to it?

5. Write about your experience learning English. Why are you studying English? How do you feel about English? What is easy for you to understand in English? What are some difficulties you have in English?

6. Write about your favorite type of fashion in clothing. What kind is it? Why do you like it?

7. Write about an "extreme" sport, such as bungee jumping. How do you feel about this sport? Do you want to try this sport? Why or why not? Describe the types of people who enjoy these kinds of sports.

8. What do you miss about your country? Write about some things that you cannot find in the United States.

9. Write about your home. How many rooms are in your home? What color is it? How old is it? Do you like it? What is your favorite room in the home?

10. Write about what you do in your leisure (free) time. Who do you spend the time with? What activities do you do? How long do you spend doing these activities? Are your free-time activities the same during the week and on weekends?

EXTRA WRITING

Unit 2

Connecting Sentences and Paragraphs

GOAL: To learn about paragraph structure

GRAMMAR AND SENTENCE STRUCTURE: Adjectives, subject pronouns, possessive adjectives

SENTENCES: USING ADJECTIVES

You already know that a sentence must have a subject and a verb. (Remember from Unit 1 that a sentence without a subject or without a verb is called a fragment.) However, you can make a sentence much more interesting if you add descriptive words. These descriptive words are called adjectives. They describe nouns.

GRAMMAR AND SENTENCE STRUCTURE:
Word Order: Adjectives Before Nouns

Nouns are the names of people, places, or things. Examples are *teacher, doctor, student, city, park, cat, book,* and *pencil.*

Adjectives are words that describe nouns. Examples are *good* teacher, *busy* doctor, *new* student, *crowded* city, *green* park, *fat* cat, *heavy* book, and *yellow* pencil.

A simple way to combine two short sentences when there is an adjective is to put the adjective before the noun.

Two Short Sentences	Better Writing

I have a <u>cat</u>. It is <u>fat</u>.
    NOUN   ADJ.

I have a <u>fat</u> <u>cat</u>.
    ADJ.NOUN

This is my <u>car</u>. It is <u>new</u>.
    NOUN   ADJ.

This is my <u>new</u> <u>car</u>.
    ADJ. NOUN

Mr. Vicks is a <u>teacher</u>. He is <u>excellent</u>.
    NOUN   ADJ.

Mr. Vicks is an <u>excellent</u> <u>teacher</u>.
    ADJ.   NOUN

Rachel draws <u>small</u> <u>pictures</u>. Rachel draws <u>ink</u> <u>pictures</u>.
    ADJ.   NOUN   ADJ.   NOUN

Rachel draws <u>small</u> <u>ink</u> <u>pictures</u>.
    ADJ. ADJ. NOUN

Careful! Be sure to put the adjective before the noun, not after.

Incorrect: I have a car red with a top gray.

Correct: I have a red car with a gray top.

Incorrect: We ate salad chicken with potatoes fried.

Correct: We ate chicken salad with fried potatoes.

Careful! Adjectives do not have a plural form to describe plural nouns.

Incorrect: There are rares books in the library.

Correct: There are rare books in the library.

Incorrect: Do you like populars songs?

Correct: Do you like popular songs?

(See Appendix 12 for more about order of adjectives.)

Editing

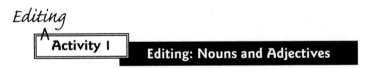

Activity 1   **Editing: Nouns and Adjectives**

Combine the following sentences. You will have to eliminate a few words. Remember to use a capital letter at the beginning and a period at the end. The first one has been done for you.

1. Robert owns a Ferrari. The Ferrari is red.

    Robert owns a red Ferrari.

2. I don't like this weather. The weather is humid.

3. Paris is a city in France. This city is beautiful.

   _____

4. Ali has a job. The job is part-time.

   _____

5. They like to drink cola. The cola is diet.

   _____

6. Marian reads folk tales. They are international.

   _____

7. My mother grows roses. The roses are big. The roses are beautiful.

   _____

8. Gillian works for a company. The company is small. The company is independent.

   _____

9. My grandparents live in a town. The town is small. It is a farming town.

   _____

10. Sharon rents a house on Smith Street. The house is tiny. The house is gray.

   _____

GRAMMAR AND SENTENCE STRUCTURE:
Word Order: Adjectives After the Verb *Be*

You have learned that adjectives come before the noun they describe.

The <u>young boy</u> carried the <u>heavy box</u>.
     ADJ. NOUN   ADJ. NOUN

In this sentence, *young* describes boy and *heavy* describes box.

Complements

Adjectives can be used in another way. If the main verb of a sentence is a form of *be*, the adjective comes *after* the verb. The adjective is called a *complement*.

The <u>boy</u> is <u>young</u>.   The <u>box</u> is <u>heavy</u>.
   NOUN   ADJ.   NOUN   ADJ.

My <u>uncle</u> is <u>rich</u>.   <u>Paris</u> is <u>beautiful</u>.
    NOUN   ADJ.   NOUN   ADJ.

That <u>music</u> is <u>loud</u>!   <u>Jim</u> is <u>sleepy</u>.
    NOUN   ADJ.   NOUN   ADJ.

That <u>house</u> is <u>big</u>.   That <u>house</u> is <u>green</u>.   That <u>house</u> is <u>big</u> and <u>green</u>.
    NOUN   ADJ.   NOUN   ADJ.   NOUN   ADJ.   ADJ.

Adjectives are very important in writing, so be sure that you use them correctly.

Activity 2 | **Practice with Adjectives**

Read the following paragraph. There are ten adjectives in the paragraph. Underline them. If you need help finding the adjectives, look at the numbers in parentheses on the left side of the paragraph. These numbers tell you how many adjectives are in each line. The first one has been done for you.

Paragraph 4

EXAMPLE PARAGRAPH

My Dream Vacation

(2)   I have a dream to visit Alaska. The weather is <u>beautiful</u> there. I love cold weather.

(1)   When the temperature is low, I have energy! I also want to visit Alaska because I

(3)   love nature. Alaska is **pure** and natural. I dream about the beautiful landscape. In

(1)   addition, there are wild

      animals. Finally, I want

(1)   to learn important infor-

(1)   mation about the **native**

      people of Alaska. I hope

(1)   to visit beautiful Alaska

      soon.

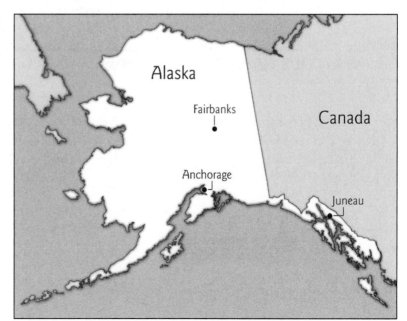

pure: clean; not polluted

native: born in a certain place; originated

WHAT IS A PARAGRAPH?

In Unit 1, you studied sentences. A **sentence** is a group of words that expresses a complete thought. You learned that a sentence has two main parts: the subject and the verb. The words in a sentence are in a special order.

Most people write much more than one sentence. Sometimes they write a paragraph. A **paragraph** is a group of sentences. All of the sentences in a paragraph are about one specific topic. (Note: After you study paragraphs in this book, you can study and practice them further in *Great Paragraphs*.)

> A paragraph has two main parts: the topic sentence and the body. The body includes supporting sentences and a concluding sentence.

The **topic sentence** is one sentence that tells the main idea of the whole paragraph. This sentence is often found at the beginning of the paragraph.

The **body** of a paragraph has sentences with information that supports the topic sentence. It is important to remember that *every* sentence in the body must be connected in some way to the topic sentence.

In addition to the topic sentence and the body, some paragraphs have a third part: a **concluding sentence**. The concluding sentence is the end of the paragraph. It is a brief summary of the information in the paragraph. Many paragraphs, especially short paragraphs, do not have a concluding sentence.

WORKING WITH THE WHOLE PARAGRAPH

Let's see how the parts of a paragraph work together to make a good paragraph that is easy to read.

WRITER'S NOTE: Topic Sentence

Every good paragraph has a topic sentence. If there is no topic sentence, the reader may be confused because the ideas will not be organized clearly. When you write a paragraph, remember to use a topic sentence. It gives the general topic of the whole paragraph.

Activity 3 **Paragraph Study**

Read the following two paragraphs. Answer the questions that follow.

Paragraph 5

My Favorite Color

My favorite color is blue. I have six blue shirts. I wear blue jeans almost every day. I have a pair of light blue tennis shoes. I own a blue car, and my computer is blue. Other colors are nice, but I like blue the best.

1. How many sentences are in this paragraph? _____

2. What is the main topic of this paragraph? (Circle the letter of the answer.)

    a. The writer likes blue computers.

    b. The writer likes blue.

    c. The writer likes light blue clothes.

3. What is the topic sentence? Remember that the topic sentence tells the main idea of the whole paragraph. Write it here:

    _____

4. The writer gives five examples of blue things. What five blue things does the writer have? Write five sentences about these blue things. Follow the example.

    a. _The writer has six blue shirts._____

    b. _____

    c. _____

    d. _____

    e. _____

5. Sometimes paragraphs have a concluding sentence. A concluding sentence is a summary of the ideas in the paragraph. If there is a concluding sentence, write it here:

    _____

6. Read the paragraph again. Can you find at least two descriptive adjectives? Write them below.

    _____

Paragraph 6

The Franklin Building

EXAMPLE PARAGRAPH

   I work in an interesting building. This building is in **downtown** Atlanta. The name of the building is the Franklin Building. It is dark red. It is made of **brick**. It has many windows. The building has six **floors**. Each floor has a different company. Everyone likes the Franklin Building very much.

downtown: the center of a city (usually commercial/cultural)   **floors:** levels of a building

brick: small squares of baked clay used to build houses and buildings

1. How many sentences are in this paragraph?

   _____

2. What is the main topic of this paragraph? (Circle the letter of the answer.)

   a. information about a city

   b. information about a person

   c. information about a building

3. What is the topic sentence? Remember that the topic sentence tells the main idea of the whole paragraph. Write it here:

   _____

   _____

   _____

   _____

   _____

   _____

   _____

4. Answer these questions in complete sentences.

   a. Where is the building?

    _____

   b. What is the name of the building?

    _____

   c. What color is the building?

    _____

   d. How many floors does the building have?

    _____

5. Sometimes paragraphs have a concluding sentence. A concluding sentence is a summary of the ideas in the paragraph. If there is a concluding sentence, write it here:

_____

_____

6. Read the paragraph again. Can you find at least four descriptive adjectives? Write them below.

_____

_____

WRITER'S NOTE: Indent the First Line of Every Paragraph

Look at the first line of Paragraph 5 on page 35. How is the formatting different from the other lines in the paragraph?

Look at the first line of Paragraph 6 on page 36. Do you see how the first line is also moved in? The name for this space is called an indentation. The action of making this space at the beginning of a paragraph is to **indent**.

It is important to indent the first line of every paragraph. Don't forget to indent!

Activity 4	Copying a Paragraph

On the lines below, copy the five sentences about spaghetti from Activity 3, Unit 1, page 7. Be sure to indent the first line. Use correct punctuation at the end of each sentence. Give this paragraph a title. When you finish, read your new paragraph. Underline the topic sentence.

Paragraph 7

_____

_____

_____

_____

_____

_____

_____

_____

_____

_____

On the lines below, copy the eight sentences about the taxi driver from Activity 5, Unit 1, pages 8–9. Be sure to indent the first line. Use correct punctuation at the end of each sentence. Give this paragraph a title. When you finish, read your new paragraph. Underline the topic sentence.

Paragraph 8

_____

_____

_____

_____

_____

_____

_____

_____

Activity 5   **Writing an Original Paragraph**

Answer the questions. Be sure to use complete sentences. When you finish, write your sentences in paragraph form on the lines provided below.

1. Who is your favorite singer? My favorite singer is _____

2. What country does he/she come from? _____

   _____

3. What kind of music does he/she sing? _____

   _____

4. What is your favorite song by this singer? _____

5. Why do you like this singer? _____

   _____

Now write your sentences in paragraph form. Be sure to give your paragraph a title.

_____

_____

_____

_____

_____

_____

_____

_____

_____

WORKING WITH TOPIC SENTENCES

Every paragraph must have a good topic sentence. The topic sentence gives the main idea of the paragraph. The topic sentence should not be too specific or too general. The topic sentence tells the reader what the paragraph is about.

Activity 6   **Topic Sentences**

Read each paragraph and the three topic sentences below it. Then choose the best topic sentence and write it on the line. Read the paragraph again. Make sure that the topic sentence gives the main idea for the whole paragraph. Remember to indent!

Paragraph 9

Maria and Her Great Job

_____

_____ . She works at Papa Joe's Restaurant. She serves about sixty people every day. Maria can remember all the dinner orders. If there is a problem with any of the food, she takes it back to the kitchen immediately. Maria wants every customer to have a good meal at the restaurant.

     a. My cousin Maria is an excellent server.
     b. My cousin Maria works at Papa Joe's Restaurant.
     c. Maria's customers do not eat big meals.

Paragraph 10

My Favorite City

_____

_____ . I love to see all the interesting things there. The city is big, exciting, and full of life. I always visit the Empire State Building and the Statue of Liberty. I also visit Chinatown. At night, I go to a **show** on Broadway. The food in the city is excellent, too. I truly enjoy New York City.

show: live performance on stage

     a. I like to see the Empire State Building and the Statue of Liberty.
     b. New York is a very big city.
     c. My favorite city in the world is New York City.

Paragraph 11

Is Snow Really Beautiful?

_____

_____ . Snow is beautiful when it falls. After a few days, the snow isn't beauti-

ful anymore. It starts to melt. The clean streets become **messy**. It is difficult to walk anywhere.

The **sidewalks** are slippery. Snow often causes **traffic** problems. Some roads are closed. Other

roads are hard to drive on safely. Drivers have more **accidents** on snowy roads. I understand why

some people like snow, but I don't like it very much.

messy: sloppy; dirty   **traffic:** cars and other vehicles
sidewalks: paved walkways on the side of roads   **accidents:** car crashes

    a. In December, it usually snows.
    b. Some people like snow, but I don't.
    c. I love snow.

Activity 7   **More Work with Topic Sentences**

*Read each paragraph and the four topic sentences below it. Then choose the best topic sentence
and write it on the line. Read the paragraph again. Make sure that the topic sentence gives the
main idea for the whole paragraph. Be sure to indent!*

Paragraph 12

Pasta, Pasta, Pasta

_____

_____ . Pasta tastes great. Sometimes I eat it **plain**. I also like it with butter

or **parmesan** cheese. Another reason I like pasta is the **variety**. Pasta includes spaghetti,

macaroni, vermicelli, ravioli, lasagna, and many other kinds. In addition, pasta is really easy to

prepare. I can make pasta in less than 15 minutes. Finally, pasta is a very healthy food for

me. A plate of pasta has about 300 **calories**, but it has only 3 grams of fat. I want to eat

pasta every day!

plain: with nothing added; simple   **variety:** many different kinds
parmesan: a hard, dry Italian cheese   **calories:** measurement of heat energy of food

a. Everybody loves pasta.

b. Spaghetti and macaroni are kinds of pasta.

c. Pasta is my favorite food.

d. Pasta comes from Italy.

Paragraph 13

Good Teachers

_____

_____ . First of all, good teachers are **patient**. They never rush their students. Good teachers explain things without getting **bored**. In addition, they are organized. They plan what happens in every class. Good teachers are also **encouraging**. They help students understand the subject. Finally, good teachers are fair. They treat all students the same. These are some of the most important qualities of good teachers.

patient: calm; untiring   **bored:** not interested   **encouraging:** helpful; comforting

a. All good teachers are patient.

b. Good teachers have special qualities.

c. I like my teachers.

d. Some teachers are good, but some teachers are not so good.

Paragraph 14

A Radio Station for Everyone

_____

_____ . Radio Station 97.5 FM plays Spanish music. For people who like rock music, there is Station 98.1. The music on Radio Station 101.5 is all jazz. Station 103.6 plays blues music during the day and jazz at night. Station 103.9 plays many different kinds of music. Station 105.7 plays dance music for young people. This city is lucky to have so many kinds of music stations.

a. This city offers radio stations for everyone.

b. This city does not have many Spanish music stations.

c. I do not like rock music very much.

d. I like jazz a lot.

GRAMMAR AND SENTENCE STRUCTURE:
Subject Pronouns

A pronoun is a word that takes the place of a noun. A subject pronoun comes before the verb, just like any subject usually does. In English, there are seven subject pronouns.

Singular	**Plural**
I	we
you	you
he / she / it	they

Examples with sentences:

Singular	**Plural**
I live in Panama.	We live in Panama.
You are from Africa.	You are from Africa.
He works in a factory.	They work in a factory.

Activity 8   **Subject Pronouns**

Read the following paragraph. Replace the nouns in parentheses with a subject pronoun. The first one has been done for you.

Paragraph 15

Two Doctors

Rosemarie Bertrand is a doctor in Edinburgh, Scotland. (**1.** Rosemarie Bertrand)

___She_____ is married to Michael Scott. (**2.** Michael Scott) _____ is also

a doctor. (**3.** Rosemarie and Michael) _____ live in Edinburgh. (**4.** Edinburgh)

_____ is a beautiful city. Dr. Bertrand and Dr. Scott have an office together

downtown. (**5.** The office) _____ is busy every day. (**6.** Rosemarie and Michael)

_____ work hard five days a week. On weekends, however, (**7.** Rosemarie and

Michael) _____ like to travel to the countryside. (**8.** The countryside)

_____ is beautiful and relaxing.

WRITER'S NOTE:
Writing About People: Proper Nouns and Subject Pronouns

When you write about a person, you use that person's name. The name is called a proper noun. (For more information about proper nouns, see p. 9.) Study these examples:

<u>George Woods</u> teaches at Briar Elementary School. <u>He</u> teaches math and science there.
    NOUN   PRONOUN

<u>Alisa</u> lives in the city. <u>She</u> likes the noise and the crowds.
NOUN   PRONOUN

It is correct to use a person's name when you write one or two sentences, but in a paragraph or in conversation, good writers and speakers do not use the person's name many times. Instead, they can use a subject **pronoun** (*I*, *you*, *he*, *she*, *it*, *we*, and *they*).

Remember: Do not repeat the proper noun many times. Replace it with a pronoun.

WORKING WITH THE BODY OF THE PARAGRAPH

Earlier in this unit you practiced topic sentences. Every topic sentence must have supporting sentences—these make up the body of the paragraph. This body of supporting sentences is directly related to the topic sentence. Supporting sentences give information about the topic sentence. Therefore, the supporting sentences are just as important as the topic sentence.

One mistake that many writers make is writing sentences that are not related to the topic sentence. Plan what your supporting information will be so it is related to the topic sentence.

WRITER'S NOTE:
Supporting Sentences: The Body of a Paragraph

You have learned that a paragraph has two main parts: the topic sentence and the body. The body consists of sentences that give supporting information and ideas about the topic sentence. Therefore, it is important for *every* sentence to be directly related to the topic sentence.

Make sure that each sentence provides support, details, or examples for the ideas in the topic sentence. Throw out any unrelated or unconnected ideas!

Activity 9	The Body of the Paragraph

Read each paragraph carefully. Circle the topic sentence. In each paragraph, one supporting sentence does not belong because it is not directly connected to the topic sentence. It does not fit the ideas in the paragraph. Draw a line under the sentence that does not belong.

Paragraph 16

EXAMPLE PARAGRAPH

Keeping Score in American Football

Keeping **score** in American football is more difficult than keeping score in soccer. In soccer, each goal is **worth** one point. For example, if a team scores five goals in a game, then the team's score is five points. In American football, the scoring system is different. When a player carries the ball across the end zone, he scores a touchdown. A touchdown is worth six points. When a player kicks the football between the goal posts, then that team gets one point or three points. Another sport that has easy scoring is basketball.

score: total; count
worth: equal to; valued at

Paragraph 17

EXAMPLE PARAGRAPH

Celsius and Fahrenheit Temperatures

Changing temperatures from Celsius to Fahrenheit is not difficult. First, **multiply** the Celsius temperature by 9. Then **divide** this answer by 5. When you finish, add 32 **degrees** to your answer. The result is the temperature in Fahrenheit. Many countries report temperatures in Celsius, but the United States uses Fahrenheit. For example, if the Celsius temperature is 20, you multiply 20 by 9. Then you divide the answer, 180, by 5. The result is 36. Next, add 32, and you have the correct Fahrenheit temperature. Now you know how to change a temperature from Celsius to Fahrenheit.

multiply: 2 x 2 = 4
divide: 15 ÷ 3 = 5
degrees: units of measurement for temperature: 98° = 98 degrees

Paragraph 18

Making **Chili**

Chili is an easy and delicious dish to prepare. Fried chicken is also easy to prepare. To make chili, cut up two large onions. Then fry them in a little vegetable oil. You can add fresh garlic and some **diced** chili peppers. When the onions are soft, add two pounds of **ground** beef. **Stir** the onions and beef until they are **fully** cooked. Sprinkle one table-spoon of red chili powder on top. Next, add four cups of diced tomatoes and two cups of water. After that, add one can of red beans. Finally, add salt and pepper. Cover the saucepan and cook over low heat for about one hour. If you follow this easy **recipe**, you will have a delicious **meal**!

chili: a thick stew made with meat, beans, and tomatoes
diced: cut into little squares
ground: broken into small pieces
stir: mix
fully: completely; entirely
recipe: directions for cooking food
meal: breakfast, lunch, or dinner

GRAMMAR AND SENTENCE STRUCTURE:
Possessive Adjectives

When you want to talk about something that belongs to someone or something, you use a possessive adjective. A possessive adjective shows possession. Whose house? Whose books? Whose television?

In English, there are seven **possessive adjectives**: *my, your, his, her, its, our, their.* A possessive adjective always comes before a noun.

my	I live in <u>my</u> father's house.
your	Do you have <u>your</u> books?
his	He lives with <u>his</u> father.
her	She does not carry money in <u>her</u> purse.
its	Poor cat! It has a cut on <u>its</u> face.
our	We write all <u>our</u> papers on a computer.
their	They can bring <u>their</u> CDs.

Activity 10 — Possessive Adjectives

Read the following paragraph. Write the missing possessive adjectives. The first one has been done for you.

Paragraph 19

Caroline and Her Sisters

Caroline has two sisters and one brother. (**1.**) _Their_____ names are Ashley, Margaret, and Nick. Ashley and Margaret live with (**2.**) _____ parents. They are high school students. Ashley likes to play sports. (**3.**) _____ favorite sport is softball. She is a very good player. Margaret does not like sports, but she loves music. She plays (**4.**) _____ guitar every afternoon after school. Ashley and Margaret have the same friends. (**5.**) _____ friends go to the same school. (**6.**) _____ brother Nick is in college. (**7.**) _____ major is business administration. Caroline is only ten years old, and she loves (**8.**) _____ family very much.

Activity 11	Subject Pronouns and Possessive Adjectives

This paragraph contains many subject pronouns and possessive adjectives. Underline the correct forms in parentheses ( ). The first one has been done for you.

Paragraph 20

(I, <u>My</u>) Grandmother

A very important person in (**1.** I, my) life is (**2.** I, my) grandmother. (**3.** She, Her) name is Evelyn Anna Kratz. (**4.** She, Her) life is very interesting. (**5.** She, Her) is 89 years old. (**6.** She, Her) comes from Poland. (**7.** She, Her) can speak English well, but (**8.** she, her) first language is Polish. My grandmother comes from a large family. (**9.** She, Her) has two brothers. (**10.** They, Their) names are Peter and John. (**11.** I, My) grandmother has two sisters, too. (**12.** They, Their) names are Karina and Maria. (**13.** I, My) like to listen to (**14.** my, her) grandmother's stories because (**15.** they, their) are so interesting. In (**16.** I, my) opinion, they are the most interesting stories in the world.

Activity 12	More Practice with the Body of the Paragraph

Read the topic sentence and body of each paragraph carefully. In each paragraph, there are two sentences that do not belong. Find and underline these sentences.

Paragraph 21

The "New" States

Four of the U.S. states begin with the word "New." New Hampshire, New Jersey, and New York are in the Northeast, but New Mexico is in the Southwest. Arizona is also in the Southwest. New Hampshire is a small state with about one million people. New Jersey is also a small state, but its population is about eight million people. The most **well-known** of the "New" states is New York. The population of New York is about twenty million. New Mexico is the largest of these four states, but its population is small. There are no states that begin with the word "Old." Although all these states begin with "New," they are all very different.

well-known: popular, familiar, famous

Paragraph 22

An **Incredible** Neighbor

My neighbor, Mrs. Wills, is an **amazing** person. She is 96 years old. My grandmother lived to be 87. Mrs. Wills lives alone, and she takes care of herself. In the morning, she works in her garden. It is certainly a very beautiful garden. She also does all of her own cooking. She does not like to cook rice. She cleans her own house. She even puts her heavy garbage can by the street for trash collection. She pulls the can slowly to the **curb**. She goes up and down the steps to her door. I hope to have that much energy and ability when I am 96 years old.

incredible: difficult to believe, amazing, surprising
amazing: remarkable; wonderful
curb: side of the street

Paragraph 23

My Office

My office is a comfortable place to work. On the left side of the room, there is a big **wooden** desk. My computer sits on top of the desk, and the printer sits under the desk. I keep paper **files** in the drawers. On the right side of the room, there are two beautiful bookcases. My father makes bookcases and other wood furniture. These bookcases are full of books, magazines, and computer software. There is also a telephone and a fax machine in my office. I have trouble remembering my telephone number. There is a closet next to the fax machine. All my office supplies are there. I enjoy my office very much.

wooden: made of wood   **files**: documents; papers

WRITER'S NOTE: Check for the Verb

Do you sometimes forget to include the verb in a sentence? Many writers make this mistake. This is the rule: Every sentence needs a verb.

Incorrect: My father's name Samuel.
Correct: My father's name is Samuel.

Incorrect:	Many people in Switzerland French.
Correct:	Many people in Switzerland speak French.
Incorrect:	Some elementary schools computers for the students.
Correct:	Some elementary schools have computers for the students.

When you check your writing, look at each sentence carefully. Is there a verb? Remember that every sentence needs a verb.

Editing

Activity 13   **Editing: Checking for Verbs**

Read this paragraph. Five sentences are missing the verb be. *Find these five sentences and then add the correct form of the* be *verb. The first one is done for you.*

Paragraph 24

Staying Healthy

It ~is~ easy to stay healthy if you **follow** some simple steps. First, think about the food you eat. The best types of food fruits and vegetables. It important to eat a lot of them every day. Next, **consider** some exercise. Doctors say that one hour of **moderate** exercise each day can keep you in good shape. In addition, exercise good for the body and the mind. Finally, relaxation very important. Take time to **appreciate** the good things in life. You can follow these steps to help yourself stay healthy.

follow: obey; do
steps: directions
consider: think about
moderate: an average amount
appreciate: enjoy

WORKING WITH CONCLUDING SENTENCES

You learned about topic sentences and body sentences. All good paragraphs have a topic sentence. The topic sentence is usually (but not always) the first sentence in a paragraph. All paragraphs have a body that contains several sentences. These sentences must relate to the topic sentence.

A paragraph may end with another part called the concluding sentence. The concluding sentence often gives a summary of the information in the paragraph. In many cases, the information in the topic sentence is similar to the information in the concluding sentence.

Look at the topic sentences and concluding sentences from these paragraphs in this unit.

	Paragraph 4, Page 33	**Paragraph 5, Page 35**	**Paragraph 6, Page 36**
Topic Sentence	I have a dream to visit Alaska.	My favorite color is blue.	I work in an interesting building.
Concluding Sentence	I hope to visit beautiful Alaska soon.	Other colors are nice, but I like blue the best.	Everyone likes the Franklin Building very much.

Activity 14 | **Concluding Sentences**

Copy the topic sentence and the concluding sentence from each paragraph indicated. How are the two sentences the same? How are they different? Discuss with a partner.

1. Paragraph 9, p. 41

   Topic sentence: _____

   Concluding sentence: _____

2. Paragraph 10, p. 41

   Topic sentence: _____

   Concluding sentence: _____

3. Paragraph 11, p. 42

   Topic sentence: _____

   Concluding sentence: _____

4. Paragraph 12, p. 42

Topic sentence: _____

Concluding sentence: _____

5. Paragraph 13, p. 43

Topic sentence: _____

Concluding sentence: _____

6. Paragraph 14, p. 43

Topic sentence: _____

Concluding sentence: _____

Activity 15   **Choosing Concluding Sentences**

Read each paragraph. Then read the concluding sentences below it. Circle the letter of the best concluding sentence.

Paragraph 25

Monday

I hate Monday for many reasons. One reason is work. I get up early to go to work on Monday. After a weekend of fun and relaxation, I don't like to go to work. Another reason that I don't like Monday is that I have three meetings every Monday. These meetings last a long time. They are **extremely** boring. Traffic is also a big problem on Monday. There are more cars on the road on Monday. Drivers are in a bad **mood**, and I must be more careful than usual.

extremely: very   mood: disposition; humor

    a. Monday is worse than Tuesday, but it is better than Sunday.

    b. I don't like meetings on Monday.

    c. These are just a few reasons why I don't like Monday.

Paragraph 26

Good Luck, Bad Luck

Superstitions can mean good luck or bad luck. For example, some people believe that the number 7 is lucky. Other people think that if you see a shooting star, you can make a wish and it will come true. However, most superstitions are bad luck. **For instance**, many people believe that it is bad luck to open an umbrella inside a house. They also think that it is bad luck if a black cat walks in front of you. Other people think that if your left ear is burning, someone is saying something bad about you.

for instance: for example

    a. People believe exactly the same superstitions.

    b. Many people believe in good and bad superstitions.

    c. The worst superstition is about breaking a mirror.

Paragraph 27

Buying a Car

Buying a car **requires** careful planning. Do you want a new or a used car? This depends on how much money you can spend. What style of car do you want? You can look at many different models to help you decide. Next, do you want extra **features** in your new car? Does a used car need any repairs before you buy it? Finally, you have to decide where you will buy your car.

requires: needs   features: options, such as air-conditioning or tinted windows

    a. It is important to think about these things when you are buying a car.

    b. The most important thing is the kind of car that you want to buy.

    c. Will you buy your new car from a friend or a car dealer?

Editing

Activity 16   **Editing: Grammar and Sentence Review**

Read this paragraph. There are seven mistakes: three (3) mistakes with adjectives, two (2) missing be verbs, and two (2) capitalization mistakes. Find and correct the mistakes.

Paragraph 28

Aspirin

aspirin is an incredible medicine. This small white drug is a medicine old. We do not know

exactly why or how it works. However, millions of people use aspirin every day. we take aspirin

for reasons many. Aspirin good for headaches, colds, and pain. Aspirin can help with so many

different health problems. Aspirin is a medicine simple, but it great.

Activity 17	Original Writing Practice

Answer the following questions and write eight to ten sentences about travel. Copy your sentences into a paragraph below. Then use the checklist that follows. Put a check (✓) next to each step as you complete it.

Topic: Travel

1. What city do you want to visit? _____

2. What kind of transportation do you need to get to this city? _____

_____

3. What are some reasons to go there? Think of at least three reasons. (Use adjectives in your descriptions.)

   a. Reason 1: _____

   _____

   b. Reason 2: _____

   _____

   c. Reason 3: _____

   _____

4. List two or three special activities that you can do in this city.

   a. Activity 1: _____

   _____

   b. Activity 2: _____

   _____

   c. Activity 3 (optional): _____

   _____

5. How long do you want to stay in this city? _____

_____

6. Do you recommend this city to other people? _____

_____

Checklist

✔1. ❏ Use adjectives to describe this city.

✔2. ❏ Indent the first line of your paragraph.

✔3. ❏ Check the first sentence (topic sentence) and the last sentence (concluding sentence). Are they similar in meaning?

✔4. ❏ Check each sentence in your paragraph. Is every sentence related to your topic?

Paragraph 29

_____

_____

_____

_____

_____

_____

_____

_____

_____

Activity 18   **Peer Editing**

Exchange papers from Activity 17 with another student. Read your partner's paragraph. Use Peer Editing Sheet 2 on page 221 to help you talk about your partner's work.

Activity 19   **Journal Writing**

Here are ten ideas for journal writing. Write about as many as you can. Follow your teacher's directions. (We recommend that you skip a line after each line that you write. This gives your teacher a place to write comments.)

1. Write about New York City. What do you know about it? Do you want to visit this city? Why or why not?

2. Write about swimming or another sport. Do you like to practice this sport? How often? Why do you enjoy this sport?

3. Write about your favorite kind of music. Why do you like this music? How do you feel when you listen to this music?

4. Write about how to use a _____ . Explain the steps involved in using this thing.

5. Write about credit cards. What is your opinion about them? Are they helpful or dangerous? Do you use them?

6. Write about a good weekend plan. What do you like to do on the weekend? Who do you spend your weekends with?

7. Choose a person in your class to write about. Explain how the person looks, and what his or her personality is like.

8. Write about a famous person you like. Who is this person? What is this person's job? Why do you like this person?

9. Write about something that you do not like. Give three reasons why you do not like this thing.

10. Write about your favorite subject in school. Why do you like this subject? What kinds of things do you practice in this subject?

EXTRA WRITING

Part II

Developing Sentences

Unit 3

Writing About the Present

GOAL: To learn how to write sentences in the simple present tense

GRAMMAR AND SENTENCE STRUCTURE: Simple present tense; object pronouns

SENTENCE DEVELOPMENT: Compound sentences

BEGIN WITH THE PRESENT TENSE

When you write about daily habits and activities or things that are generally true, use the present tense.

GRAMMAR AND SENTENCE STRUCTURE:
Simple Present Tense: Statements and Questions

In English, the present tense can be divided into two categories: regular verbs and the verbs *be* and *have*. Do you know the following verb forms?

Present Tense Verb Forms: Statements

Verb *be*	I **am**	we **are**
	you **are**	you (plural) **are**
	he / she / it **is**	they **are**

Verb *have*	I **have**	we **have**
	you **have**	you (plural) **have**
	he / she / it **has**	they **have**
Verb *live* (regular)	I **live**	we **live**
	you **live**	you (plural) **live**
	he / she / it **lives**	they **live**
Verb *go* (regular)	I **go**	we **go**
	you **go**	you (plural) **go**
	he / she / it **goes**	they **go**

Present Tense Verb Forms: Questions

Verb *be*	**Am** I . . . ?	**Are** we . . . ?
	Are you . . . ?	**Are** you (plural) . . . ?
	Is he / she / it . . . ?	**Are** they . . . ?
Verb *have*	**Do** I have . . . ?	**Do** we have . . . ?
	Do you have . . . ?	**Do** you (plural) have . . . ?
	Does he / she / it have . . . ?	**Do** they have . . . ?
Verb *live*	**Do** I live . . . ?	**Do** we live . . . ?
	Do you live . . . ?	**Do** you (plural) live . . . ?
	Does he / she / it live . . . ?	**Do** they live . . . ?
Verb *go*	**Do** I go . . . ?	**Do** we go . . . ?
	Do you go . . . ?	**Do** you (plural) go . . . ?
	Does he / she / it go . . . ?	**Do** they go . . . ?

NOTE: All verbs except *be* must add *do* or *does* to make a question.

In this unit, you will practice writing sentences and paragraphs in the present tense.

WRITER'S NOTE: Using Contractions

A **contraction** is a short version of a pronoun and a verb combined, such as *I am / I'm*. The apostrophe (') shows where a letter has been left out. Here are some common contractions with *be*:

I am = I'm	we are = we're
you are = you're	you (plural) are = you're
he is = he's / she is = she's / it is = it's	they are = they're

Some people believe contractions are too informal for academic writing. Be sure to ask your instructor if using contractions is acceptable.

| Activity 1 | Present Tense Forms |

Read each sentence. Write the correct form of the verb in parentheses.

Paragraph 30

Uncle Charlie

My Uncle Charlie (**1.** be) _____ a wonderful man. He (**2.** be)

_____ an entrepreneur. He began his restaurant business ten years ago. Now he

enjoys great success. In his restaurant, he (**3.** have) _____ ten waiters, two

managers, and three chefs. Uncle Charlie (**4.** work) _____ very hard in his

restaurant. Sometimes he is there seven days a week. He and his wife Valerie always (**5.** go)

_____ to the restaurant at night to make sure that the customers are happy. I (**6.**

love) _____ Uncle Charlie and Aunt Valerie, and I really appreciate all their hard

work. (**7.** You / know) _____ somebody like my uncle?

| Activity 2 | The Verb *Be* in the Present |

Read this paragraph from Giacomo to his new classmate. Fill in the missing be *verbs.*

Paragraph 31

My Classmates

My classmates come from all over the world. José (**1.**) _____ from Spain, so

he speaks Spanish very well. Kuniko and Yasuhiro (**2.**) _____ Japanese, but they

don't sit next to each other in class. Yuri (**3.**) _____ from Ukraine, and he plays

soccer very well. The Al-Ahmad brothers (**4.**) _____ from Saudi Arabia, and they

(**5.**) _____ both very nice. Me? I (**6.**) _____ from Italy, and I love to

sing in class. We (**7.**) _____ all very good friends, and I hope we can be friends

forever. Where (**8.**) _____ you from?

Activity 3 | **Verbs: Changing Singular to Plural**

Read the following paragraph. Make the following changes and rewrite the paragraph on the lines.

1. *Change the subject of the story, Jim, to Jim and Billy.*
2. *You will have to make certain changes to the verb forms and to some nouns and pronouns, too.*

Paragraph 32

EXAMPLE PARAGRAPH

Jim's Daily Routine

Jim is a very busy student. He studies engineering at City College. Every day he wakes up at 7:00 in the morning, takes a shower, and then rushes off to school. He goes to school for six hours. After school, he goes to the local mall where he works in a sporting goods store. After this part-time job, he goes home, eats a quick dinner, studies, and does his homework. Jim knows that this lifestyle is stressful. He also knows that it will end soon, and he will get a professional job.

Jim and Billy's Daily Routine

Jim and Billy are very busy students.

_____

_____

_____

_____

_____

_____

Activity 4 | **Writing a Paragraph from Pictures**

Study the following pictures. They tell a story. Then read the incomplete paragraph. Some present tense verbs are missing. Fill in the blanks based on the pictures. Write the full sentence for the last two sentences. Note: The numbers in the paragraph correspond to the pictures.

Paragraph 33

One Family's Morning Routine

The Lee family is very busy on weekday mornings. (**1.**) Every morning Susan Lee, the

youngest daughter, wakes up and _____ for her parents and

siblings. She loves to cook! (**2.**) When breakfast is ready, the rest of the family _____ .

The kids eat breakfast quickly. (**3.**) After they eat, Susan's father and mother

_____ . (**4.**) At 8:30 A.M., Mr. Lee

_____ (**5.**) Then he and the kids

_____ to Mrs. Lee. (**6.**) Mr. Lee and

the kids _____ the **minivan** so that he can take them to school. (**7.**)

_____ . (**8.**) A

few minutes later, _____ .

siblings: brothers and/or sisters   minivan: a large family car, usually with sliding doors

Editing

| Activity 5 | **Editing: Subjects and Verbs** |

Read the following paragraph. There are seven errors. Most of the sentences are missing either the subject or the verb. Write the corrections above the errors. The first one has been done for you.

Paragraph 34

The City of Budapest

is
Budapest one of the most interesting capitals of Europe. Is a romantic city, and it has many
                Λ
interesting tourist places to visit. One example the Danube River. It separates Budapest into

Buda and Pest. In addition, visitors Hungarian traditional food. The most popular food goulash

soup. The people of Budapest friendly and helpful to tourists. When travel to Europe, you can

visit Budapest and have a very good time.

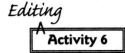

Editing

| Activity 6 | Editing: Capitalization Review |

You studied capitalization in Unit 1. Read the following paragraph about the TOEFL exam. There are ten errors in capitalization. Can you find them all? Circle the capitalization errors and write the corrections above the circled words. The first one has been done for you.

Paragraph 35

The TOEFL

Do you know about the TOEFL? It is the Test of English as a Foreign Language. Most

U

international students who want to study at a university in the (united) states take this test. it

measures english language ability. The test comes from Educational Testing Service in new

jersey. It is a very long test. the computer version of the TOEFL contains four tasks: Listening

Comprehension, Structure, Reading Comprehension, and Essay Writing. if you want to study in

the united states, it is important to prepare for this test and get a high score.

NEGATIVES AND THE PRESENT TENSE

Good writers can use the negative form of the present tense. This section gives you practice with negatives.

GRAMMAR AND SENTENCE STRUCTURE: Present Tense Verb Forms: Negatives

Verb *be*	I am **not**	we **are** **not**
	you **are** **not**	you (plural) **are** **not**
	he / she / it **is** **not**	they **are** **not**

NOTE: Some contractions are possible with the verb *be* in negative forms.

is not = isn't   are not = aren't

Verb *have*	I **do not** have	we **do not** have
	you **do not** have	you (plural) **do not** have
	he / she / it **does not** have	they **do not** have

Verb *live*   I **do not** live   we **do not** live

you **do not** live   you (plural) **do not** live

he / she / it **does not** live   they **do not** live

Verb *go*   I **do not** go   we **do not** go

you **do not** go   you (plural) **do not** go

he / she / it **does not** go   they **do not** go

NOTE: Contractions are possible with negative forms of regular verbs.

do not go = don't go   does not go = doesn't go

Activity 7   **Affirmative and Negative**

Read the sentences. Change the verb from the positive to the negative. Write the contraction form in addition. The first one has been done for you.

1. I have (contraction) a car. _I do not (OR don't) have a car._____

2. New York City is in California. _____

3. The capital of Japan is Osaka. _____

4. George goes to the library every day. _____

5. Sharks are mammals. _____

6. Irene and Julie are roommates. _____

7. Charlie works at a gas station. _____

8. My brother is a hockey player. _____

9. The teacher wants a new computer. _____

10. Alice bakes cookies often. _____

SENTENCES WITH OBJECT PRONOUNS

In Unit 2 you studied subject pronouns. Object pronouns have different forms that you need to learn.

GRAMMAR AND SENTENCE STRUCTURE:
Object Pronouns

You learned that a pronoun is a word that takes the place of a noun.

After Verbs

An object pronoun usually comes after a verb. In English, there are seven object pronouns.

Singular	**Plural**
me	us
you	you
him / her / it	them

Examples:

Singular	**Plural**
Mona likes <u>me</u>.	Mona likes <u>us</u>.
Do I know <u>you</u>?	Do I know <u>you</u>?
Karen doesn't understand <u>him</u>.	Karen doesn't understand <u>them</u>.

After Prepositions

An **object pronoun** can also come after a preposition. A **preposition** is a word that shows location, time, or direction. Some common prepositions are *to*, *with*, and *at*. Other prepositions include: *on, in, for, by, near, under, from.*

Examples:

Singular	**Plural**
Assad walks with <u>me</u>.	Assad walks with <u>us</u>.
Can I give the message to <u>you</u>?	Can I give the message to <u>you</u>?
Jane gazes at <u>him</u>.	Jane gazes at <u>them</u>.

Activity 8   Object Pronouns

Read the following paragraph. Replace the proper nouns in parentheses with an object pronoun. The first one has been done for you.

Paragraph 36

My Best Friend

My best friend is Gretchen. I met (**1.** Gretchen) <u>her</u> ten years ago. She is from Alabama.

She comes from a very large family. She has four brothers and three sisters. She doesn't live with

(**2.** her brothers and sisters) _____ . They live in Alabama with their parents.

Gretchen studies veterinary medicine at the University of Florida in Gainesville. She loves (**3.**

Gainesville) _____ very much. She also enjoys animals. Gretchen has three pets.

She has a cat. She also has a small dog. Gretchen's third pet is a large boa constrictor. She likes

(**4.** her pets) _____ all very much. In her free time, Gretchen plays tennis, reads

books, and cooks gourmet meals. I love (**5.** Gretchen) _____ like a sister. I hope

that our friendship will stay with (**6.** Gretchen and me) _____ for many years.

Activity 9	Possessive Adjective Review: Interviewing a Classmate

Find out the answers to these questions. Ask your classmate. Then write down the answers. Use
he *or* she *in the answers. Follow the example.*

Example:

What is your classmate's name? His name is Alberto. _____

1. What is your classmate's name? _____

2. Where is your classmate from? _____

3. How big is your classmate's family? _____

4. Why is your classmate in this class? _____

5. What job does your classmate want to do in the future? _____

_____

Activity 10	Writing Information in Paragraph Form

*Write the information about your classmate (from Activity 9) in the form of a paragraph. If you
need some help in organization, review Paragraph 36 in Activity 8.*

_____

_____

_____

_____

_____

_____

_____

_____

SENTENCE TYPES: SIMPLE AND COMPOUND

All the sentences you have written in the activities up to now have been simple sentences. As you learned in Unit 1, a simple sentence has a subject and a verb. Good writers often combine two simple sentences into one longer sentence. The longer sentence is called a compound sentence.

Simple and Compound Sentences

Simple Sentences

A simple sentence usually has one subject and one verb.

Japan imports oil from Saudi Arabia.

However, a simple sentence can have more than one subject and more than one verb in these combinations:

2 subjects + 1 verb: Japan and Germany import oil from Saudi Arabia.
                              SUBJECTS   +   VERB

1 subject + 2 verbs: Japan imports oil and exports cars.
                         SUBJECT   +   VERBS

2 subjects + 2 verbs: Japan and Germany import oil and export cars.
                       SUBJECTS   +   VERBS

Notice that all of these sentences have one basic subject-verb combination.

SENTENCE DEVELOPMENT

SENTENCE DEVELOPMENT

Compound Sentences

A compound sentence is two sentences joined by a connecting word, such as *and*, *but*, or *so*. A compound sentence has two subjects and two verbs:

Japan imports oil, and Saudi Arabia imports vegetables.
SUBJECT + VERB #1   SUBJECT + VERB #2

Sue watched TV, and Ben wrote letters.
SUBJECT + VERB #1   SUBJECT + VERB #2

NOTE: Compound sentences *always* use a comma (,) and a connecting word (*and*, *but*, *so*) to connect two sentences.

| Activity 11 | Sentence Types |

Read each sentence. Write S or C to show if it is simple or compound. The first two have been done for you. Hint: Look for the connectors and, but, *or* so *in compound sentences.*

1. ___C___ Japan's flag is red and white, and the Canadian flag is also red and white.

2. ___S___ Japan and Canada have the same two colors in their flags.

3. _____ The weather is bad, so the plane cannot take off on time.

4. _____ It is extremely hot in this room without an air conditioner.

5. _____ This map does not include the newly independent countries in Europe or Asia.

6. _____ For less than two hundred dollars, you can buy a round-trip ticket to Boston.

7. _____ The students take a test every Friday, but their scores are not very high.

8. _____ January, March, May, July, August, October, and December have thirty-one days.

9. _____ This recipe requires two cups of flour, two cups of sugar, and one cup of milk.

10. _____ Each ring costs sixty dollars, so five rings cost three hundred dollars.

11. _____ Some people prefer silver rings, but most people prefer gold rings.

12. _____ These silver and gold rings are different in weight and in price.

| Activity 12 | Simple Sentences to Compound Sentences |

Read each pair of simple sentences. Combine them into one sentence with a comma and a connecting word. Write the compound sentence on the line.

1. Mary lives in Turkey. Abdul lives in Kuwait. (but)

   _____

2. The weather was cold. I stayed indoors. (so)

   _____

3. We go to school every day. We play tennis on weekends. (and)

   _____

4. Linus and Kathy are related. They are not brother and sister. (but)

   _____

5. The restaurant manager was happy. He gave all the servers a raise. (so)

   _____

WRITER'S NOTE: Brainstorming with Questions

When you write a paragraph, sometimes it is difficult to find enough information to include. Good writers often ask questions to help them get ideas about what to write. First, think about your topic. Then imagine someone who does not know much about the topic. What questions might that person ask?

Quickly write down as many questions about the topic as you can think of. Don't worry now whether the questions sound good. Your purpose is just to make a list of questions. Later you can go back and read the questions. Then you can decide which questions are good ideas to write about.

Example:

   Topic: Writing about a popular sport

Possible questions:

   1. What is a popular sport?
   2. Why is it popular?
   3. How many people are needed to play this sport?
   4. Is the sport difficult to learn?
   5. Where (in which countries) is the sport popular?
   6 Is this sport popular on television?
   7 How much training does someone need in this sport?
   8. How old is this sport?

9. Do you need a lot of equipment to play this sport?

10. Is there a worldwide competition in this sport?

Can you think of other questions?

11. _____

12. _____

| Activity 13 | Questions and a Paragraph About Soccer |

The following paragraph about soccer answers some of the questions from the Writer's Note: Brainstorming with Questions. Review the soccer questions and read the paragraph. On the lines below, write the questions that the writer used to create the paragraph.

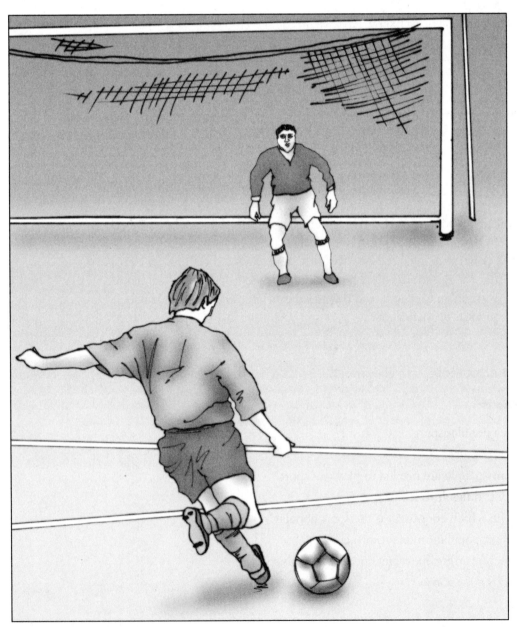

Paragraph 37

A Popular Sport

The sport of soccer is the most popular athletic activity in the world. Many people believe that this game comes from England, but others believe that it comes from the Etruscans (a group of people who lived in what is now known as Tuscany in Italy). Soccer is an international phenomenon. People all over the world play and follow this sport. Soccer is popular because it is cheap and fun. It does not require special equipment. It is also fun to watch on television. Every four years, the world enjoys watching the World Cup soccer championship. This time is probably the most exciting time for soccer teams and their fans.

Refer to pages 73–74 for the list of questions:

_____

_____

_____

_____

_____

_____

_____

Editing

| Activity 14 | **Editing: Grammar and Sentence Review** |

Read this paragraph. There are nine errors: two (2) errors with verbs, two (2) capitalization errors, two (2) adjective errors, two (2) possessive adjective errors, and one (1) subject pronoun error. Find and correct the errors. The first one has been done for you.

Paragraph 38

Not an Average Teenager

                                                                wants
Steven Mills is not a typical teenager. Steven is a gymnast, and he ~~want~~ to compete in the

olympics. He wakes up at five o'clock in the morning every day. He has a breakfast healthy. Then

she jogs to National Gymnasium on cypress Street. He practices gymnastics for two hours. Then he

gets ready for school. Steven goes to school from eight-thirty in the morning until three o'clock in

the afternoon. After school, he returns to the gymnasium for classes special with him coach. When

practice finish at six o'clock, Steven returns home. He eats dinner, does his homework, and talks

with their family. Steven is in bed by ten o'clock, so he will be ready for work the next day.

Activity 15   **Original Writing Practice**

Write a paragraph about a sport you enjoy. In your paragraph, answer these questions. Can you think of more questions? Then use the checklist below. Put a check (✓) next to each step as you complete it.

1. Which sport do you enjoy?
2. Why do you like this sport?
3. Do you play this sport? If so, how often?
4. Is the sport difficult to learn?
5. Do you like a particular athlete (or team) in this sport? Why?

Checklist

✔ 1. ❑ Make sure every sentence has a subject and a verb.

✔ 2. ❑ Make sure the verbs are in the correct tense.

✔ 3. ❑ Make sure every sentence begins with a capital letter.

✔ 4. ❑ Make sure that all the proper nouns (names, cities, countries, etc.) are capitalized.

✔ 5. ❑ Make sure every sentence ends with the correct punctuation.

✔ 6. ❑ Create a title for your paragraph.

Activity 16   **Peer Editing**

Choose someone that you work well with. Exchange papers from Activity 15 with that student. Read your partner's paragraph. Use Peer Editing Sheet 3 on page 223 to help you talk about your partner's work.

| **Activity 17** | **Journal Writing** |

Here are ten ideas for journal writing. Choose one or more of them to write about. Follow your teacher's directions. (We recommend that you skip a line after each line that you write. This gives your teacher a place to write comments.)

1. Choose a member of your family. Write a paragraph about this person. Include the person's name, age, nationality, job, hobbies, etc.

2. Write about your typical routine for a day of the week. Include the time that you usually wake up, what you eat for breakfast, what your activities are during the day, whom you spend your time with, how you enjoy the day, and what time you go to bed.

3. Write about a special city in your country. Include the name of the city, the population, the special tourist attractions, and why it is an important city for you.

4. Write about a job that you are interested in. Include the title of the job, the duties of the job, and why it is interesting to you.

5. What is your favorite web site? Write about a web site that you like. What is the address? What kind of information does it have? Why do you like it?

6. Write about your best friend. What is his/her name? Where does he/she live? What makes your friendship special?

7. Write about a restaurant that you like. What is the name of this restaurant? Why do you like it? What kind of food does it serve? What is the price range? How is it decorated?

8. Write about your favorite movie. What is the title? Who are the main actors in the movie? What is the story about? Why do you like this movie?

9. Write about a specific food that you know how to cook. What are the ingredients? Is it easy to prepare? Are the ingredients expensive?

10. Write about a type of music that you *do not* enjoy. Why don't you like it? How does it make you feel when you hear it?

EXTRA WRITING

Unit 4

Writing About the Past

GOAL: To learn how to write sentences in the past tense

GRAMMAR AND SENTENCE STRUCTURE: Past tense of *be* and regular verbs; forming questions; past tense of irregular verbs; forming the negative past tense of *be*; forming the negative past tense of other verbs

SENTENCE DEVELOPMENT: Compound sentences with *but*

BEGIN WITH THE PAST TENSE

What happened yesterday? What happened last week? When you talk about actions in the past, you use the simple past tense. Both regular verbs and irregular verbs can be in the simple past tense.

GRAMMAR AND SENTENCE STRUCTURE:
Simple Past Tense: Statements and Questions

Past Tense of *Be*

The most common verb in English, *be*, is an irregular verb. Study the simple past tense form of the verb *be*.

Verb *be*	I **was**	we **were**
	you **were**	you (plural) **were**
	he / she / it **was**	they **were**

To form questions with the verb *be* in past tense, use the forms on page 79.

78

Past Tense of *Be*: Questions

Verb *be*	**Was** I . . . ?	**Were** we . . . ?
	Were you . . . ?	**Were** you (plural) . . . ?
	Was he / she / it . . . ?	**Were** they . . . ?

Incorrect:	I am in Guatemala last year.
Incorrect:	I were in Guatemala last year.
Correct:	I was in Guatemala last year.

Incorrect:	Was Rachel and Mario at the mall yesterday?
Incorrect:	Rachel and Mario were at the mall yesterday?
Correct:	Were Rachel and Mario at the mall yesterday?

Past Tense of Regular Verbs

Forming the simple past of regular verbs is easy. Just add *-d* or *-ed* to the ends of regular verbs. (See Appendix 2 for more about the spelling of regular past tense verbs.) Study the examples below.

Verb *live*	I live<u>d</u>	we live<u>d</u>
	you live<u>d</u>	you (plural) live<u>d</u>
	he / she / it live<u>d</u>	they live<u>d</u>
Verb *visit*	I visit<u>ed</u>	we visit<u>ed</u>
	you visit<u>ed</u>	you (plural) visit<u>ed</u>
	he / she / it visit<u>ed</u>	they visit<u>ed</u>

Past Tense of Regular Verbs: Questions

Verb *live*	**Did** I **live** . . . ?	**Did** we **live** . . . ?
	Did you **live** . . . ?	**Did** you (plural) **live** . . . ?
	Did he / she / it **live** . . . ?	**Did** they **live** . . . ?

NOTE: The question form of past tense verbs is easy to make. Just use *did* to show that the sentence is in *past* tense and that it is a *question*. The main verb in questions uses the simple (base) form: *did* + subject + *verb* (no *-ed*!).

Now study these sentences for correct forms of the past tense in statements and questions.

Incorrect:	We call our parents yesterday.
Correct:	We called our parents yesterday.

Incorrect:	Do the tourists hike down the mountain last night?
Incorrect:	The tourists hiked down the mountain last night?
Correct:	Did the tourists hike down the mountain last night?

WRITER'S NOTE: Time Phrases with Past Tense

We use certain words in a sentence to help show that something happened in the past. Some of these words include:

last night   last week   this morning   yesterday   two minutes ago

You can put these words at the beginning or the end of a sentence. Avoid using these words in the middle of a sentence. Study these examples. Can you think of any others?

Incorrect:	I yesterday scratched my knee.
Correct:	Yesterday I scratched my knee.
Correct:	I scratched my knee yesterday.
Incorrect:	Did Maria last night go to the party?
Correct:	Did Maria go to the party last night?

Activity 1   Sentences with Past Tense

The verbs in these sentences are in the present tense. Rewrite the sentences and change the verbs to the past tense. The first sentence has been done for you.

1. Mary and her daughter Natalie visit the farm.

   Mary and her daughter visited the farm.
   _____

2. Mary and Natalie pet many animals.

   _____

3. They laugh at the animals.

   _____

4. Natalie really enjoys herself.

   _____

5. She likes the chickens best.

   _____

6. Natalie watches them play all morning.

   _____

7. They play with the baby goats.

_____

8. Finally, they return home.

_____

| **Activity 2** | More Work with Past Tense |

Read the paragraph and circle the ten past tense verbs. When you finish, answer the questions in complete sentences. The first one has been done for you.

Paragraph 39

Lao-Tzu and Taoism

Lao-Tzu (was) a Chinese **philosopher**. He was born in China. He lived in the Hunan **province**.

Lao-Tzu worked as a court **librarian**. The government was **corrupt**. Lao-Tzu decided to leave

his home. Before he **abandoned** the province, someone asked him to write a book about how

to live correctly. He agreed to write the book *Tao Te Ching*. It was the beginning of the

philosophy of Taoism.

philosopher: a person who studies the universe, nature, life, and morals
province: a territory in a country
librarian: someone who works with books

corrupt: dishonest
abandoned: left (He left the province.)

Information for this paragraph came from Microsoft Encarta 96 and *Simple Abundance: A Daybook of Comfort and Joy* by Sarah Ban Breathnach, published by Warner Books, Inc., 1995.

1. Who was Lao-Tzu?

   Lao-Tzu was a famous philosopher. _____

2. Where was he born?

   _____

3. What was his job?

   _____

4. What did he do before he left his home?

   _____

5. What did this book create?

   _____

<table><tr><td>**Activity 3**</td><td>**An Important Person**</td></tr></table>

Think of an important person. It can be someone famous in history. It can be a famous singer, politician, or athlete. It can be someone from your family. Answer the questions using complete sentences.

1. Who was this person?

   _____

2. Where was the person born?

   _____

3. What was the person's job?

   _____

4. Why is the person important to you? What did he or she do?

   _____

   _____

   _____

Editing

<table><tr><td>A</td><td>**Activity 4**</td><td>**Editing: Plural to Singular**</td></tr></table>

Read the paragraph. Circle all of the past tense verbs. Then follow the directions below and make changes to the paragraph. The first sentence has been done for you. (You may want to review subject pronouns and possessive adjectives in Unit 2.)

Paragraph 40

The Top of the Class

In 1992, Anthony and Marcus (were) students at the University of North Carolina. <u>They</u> were in the criminology department. <u>They</u> were excellent in <u>their</u> studies. In class, <u>they</u> answered all of <u>their</u> instructors' questions. <u>Their</u> test grades were the best, and <u>their</u> class projects were excellent. When <u>they</u> graduated in 1996, <u>they</u> finished at the top of the class. The teachers were very proud of Anthony and Marcus.

Rewrite the paragraph on the lines below and make these changes:

1. Change *Anthony and Marcus* to *Marcia*. (Note: Marcia is a woman's name.)
2. Change the underlined pronouns to go with *Marcia*.
3. Change any other words necessary (such as *students* to *student* in the first sentence).

The Top of the Class

In 1992, Marcia was a student at the University of North Carolina.

_____

_____

_____

_____

_____

_____

_____

_____

_____

| Activity 5 | Answering Questions with *Be* |

First, discuss these questions with your classmates.

1. How do deaf people communicate with each other?

2. How do blind people read?

3. Do you know anyone who is both deaf and blind?

Then read the paragraph. Answer the questions below using forms of be. *Use complete sentences. The first one has been done for you.*

Paragraph 41

EXAMPLE PARAGRAPH

Helen Keller (1880–1968)

Helen Keller is a famous American author. She was born healthy. However, when she was two years old, she became very ill. The illness made her **deaf** and **blind**. She couldn't communicate with anyone. When she was seven years old, a teacher taught her how to communicate. The teacher's name was Annie Sullivan. When Helen was twenty years old, she started college. After her graduation, she wrote thirteen books and traveled around the world. She was an incredible woman.

deaf: not able to hear   **blind**: not able to see

1. What was the blind and deaf person's name?

   The blind and deaf person's name was Helen Keller.

2. What country was she from?

   _____

3. Was she healthy or unhealthy when she was born?

   _____

4. How old was she when she became ill?

   _____

5. Who was her teacher?

   _____

6. How old was she when she learned to communicate?

   _____

7. How old was she when she went to college?

_____

8. What did she do after graduation?

_____

IRREGULAR PAST TENSE VERBS

In this unit, you have learned how to make the past tense of a regular verb—add *-d* or *-ed* to the simple form of the verb. Some verbs, however, are irregular. This means that they take a different form in the past tense.

GRAMMAR AND SENTENCE STRUCTURE:
Past Tense of Irregular Verbs

Here are some common irregular verbs. (See Appendix 3 for a complete list of common irregular past tense verbs.)

be	was/were	feel	felt	pay	paid	send	sent
buy	bought	go	went	run	ran	sit	sat
do	did	have	had	ride	rode	speak	spoke
draw	drew	leave	left	say	said	teach	taught
cut	cut	make	made	see	saw	write	wrote

NOTE: To form questions with irregular verbs, follow the rules for regular verbs on page 79. Use *did* and the simple (present tense) verb form.

There is no special rule that tells when a verb is irregular. You must memorize the past tense form when you learn the word. A dictionary will tell you when a verb is irregular. Now study these sentences for correct forms of the irregular past tense in statements and in questions.

Incorrect:	Last night I buy a new CD.
Incorrect:	Last night I buyed a new CD.
Correct:	Last night I bought a new CD.
Incorrect:	Did you left your dictionary at home?
Incorrect:	Do you left your dictionary at home?
Correct:	Did you leave your dictionary at home?

Activity 6   **Complete the Paragraph**

Read the paragraph. It is missing two sentences. Use the pictures to create a sentence for each blank. Be sure the paragraph makes sense.

Paragraph 42

A Surprising Day

Yesterday I decided to go to the beach. I looked out my window, and I did not see any clouds

in the sky. It took me about an hour to get ready. I put on my bathing suit. (1.)

_____ I also packed my

beach bag. (**2.**) _____ I

saw the rain and waited for it to stop, but it continued. Unfortunately, I stayed home yesterday.

| Activity 7 | Irregular Past Tense Verbs |

Answer the following questions. Use the irregular form of the simple past tense. Use verbs from the list in Grammar and Sentence Structure: Past Tense of Irregular Verbs on page 85. The first one has been done for you.

1. When were you born?

    I was born in 1977. _____

2. How did you feel yesterday?

    _____

3. Where did you go last weekend?

    _____

4. When did you see a movie?

    _____

5. What did you buy last week?

    _____

6. Whom did you speak with yesterday?

    _____

7. When did you leave for school this morning?

    _____

8. When did you do your homework?

    _____

GRAMMAR AND SENTENCE STRUCTURE:
Making *Be* Negative

When you want to make a sentence with *be* negative, you use the word *not*. *Not* comes after the form of *be*.

> Paula was <u>not</u> home.   The CDs were <u>not</u> in their cases.

See Grammar and Sentence Structure: Simple Past Tense: Statements and Questions on pages 78–79 for a review of the forms of *be*.

Past Tense Verb Forms: Negatives

Verb *be*	I **was not**	we **were not**
	you **were not**	you (plural) **were not**
	he / she / it **was not**	they **were not**

NOTE: Some contractions are possible with the verb *be* in negative form.

> was not = wasn't   were not = weren't

Careful! Be sure that the apostrophe (') is placed directly before the letter *t*. Remember that the apostrophe in negatives takes the place of the letter *o*.

Incorrect:	She is'nt my sister.
Correct:	She isn't my sister. (*Or:* She's not my sister.)
Incorrect:	I was'nt in class yesterday.
Correct:	I wasn't in class yesterday.

WRITER'S NOTE: Using Contractions

It is important to remember that contractions might be too informal for academic writing. Ask your instructor if using contractions in this course is acceptable.

Activity 8	**Practicing Negative *Be* Verbs in the Past**

Read the following paragraph. Write the correct form of the be verb in the blanks. Be sure to use the negative form where indicated. The first one has been done for you.

Paragraph 43

Moving to the United States

My name is Panadda, and I (**1.**) __was__ born in Thailand. I (**2.** negative)_____ the first child. My sister Suntri (**3.**) _____ born three years before I (**4.**)

_____ born. My parents (**5.** negative) _____ rich, but they (**6.**)

_____ always happy. They (**7.**) _____ hard workers. In 1995, we

moved to the United States. Everyone in my family (**8.**) _____ very excited. We

(**9.**) _____ also scared. My parents (**10.** negative) _____ able to speak

English. When we arrived, they began English classes. My sister and I started school. We (**11.**

negative) _____ comfortable in the classroom because we didn't know the

language. After a few years, we learned about the language and the culture of the United

States.

GRAMMAR AND SENTENCE STRUCTURE:
Other Negative Verbs

All other negative verbs in English are formed in the same way in the past tense. Just write *did not* and the simple verb. Look at these examples.

Verb *live* (negative past)	I **did not live**	we **did not live**
	you **did not live**	you (plural) **did not live**
	he / she / it **did not live**	they **did not live**

NOTE: Contraction: *did not* = *didn't*

Incorrect:	Ahmed no finish his homework.
Incorrect:	Ahmed no finished his homework.
Correct:	Ahmed did not (didn't) finish his homework.

| **Activity 9** | **Practicing Negative Verbs in the Past** |

Write the words as correct sentences with past tense negative verbs. The first one has been done for you.

1. Carmen / live (negative) / in Connecticut / in 1997.

   Carmen didn't live in Connecticut in 1997.

2. Shelley / study (negative) / engineering.

_____

3. Herbert's parents / visit (negative) / him last year.

_____

4. Dinosaurs / have (negative) / large brains.

_____

5. John / help (negative) / me with my homework!

_____

NEGATIVE VERB REVIEW

In this unit, you learned about past tense verbs, questions, and negatives. This activity will help you review what you have learned.

Editing

Activity 10   **Editing: Writing Negative Sentences with Contractions**

The sentences below are false. Work with a partner and rewrite each sentence, using the negative form of the verb to make the sentence true. Then write a correct sentence. Follow the example. Some verbs are regular and some are irregular. Refer to the complete list of irregular verbs in Appendix 3.

1. Winston Churchill was a leader of Mexico.

   Winston Churchill wasn't a leader of Mexico. He was a leader of Great Britain.

2. Confucius lived in Japan. _____

_____

3. Pele played basketball. _____

_____

4. The Beatles sang in Arabic. _____

_____

5. The *Titanic* sank in the Pacific Ocean. _____

_____

6. The Statue of Liberty came from Italy. _____

_____

7. Thomas Edison invented the radio. _____

_____

8. Stephen King wrote *Romeo and Juliet*. _____

_____

9. The prophet Mohammed spoke Hindi. _____

_____

10. Marilyn Monroe was an engineer. _____

_____

Activity 11   **Simple Past Tense Review**

Read the following paragraph. Change the verbs in parentheses to the past tense. Write the negative form where indicated. The first one has been done for you.

Paragraph 44

Bob's Horrible Day

Bob (**1.** have) __had__ a horrible day on Monday. First, he (**2.** be) _____

supposed to get up at 6 A.M., but his alarm clock (**3.** work, negative) _____ . He

(4. wake up) _____ at 8 A.M. There (5. be) _____ no hot water for a

shower, so he had to use cold water. After that, his car (6. start, negative) _____ ,

and he had to take the bus. When Bob (7. get) _____ to work, his boss (8. yell)

_____ at him for being late. Next, his computer (9. crash) _____ ,

and he (10. lose) _____ all of his documents. He (11. stay) _____ at

work until midnight to redo the documents. Bob (12. decide) _____ to stay home

the next day because he (13. be) _____ too tired from all his bad luck.

COMPOUND SENTENCES WITH *BUT*

One common sentence connector is *but*. This word is often used to make compound sentences. The connector *but* shows a contrast.

Compound Sentences with *But*

The connector *but* indicates a contrast between the ideas it connects. Study this example.

Two Simple Sentences	One Compound Sentence
I bought a car. John bought a truck.	I bought a car, *but* John bought a truck.

This example is a compound sentence because it is two complete sentences connected by the word *but*. It has two subjects and two verbs.

I <u>bought</u> a car, but <u>John</u> <u>bought</u> a truck
SUBJ. VERB   SUBJ.   VERB

Look at another example.

Two Simple Sentences	One Compound Sentence
She studied for the exam. She didn't pass it.	She studied for the exam, *but* she didn't pass it.

NOTE: Notice the comma before *but*. You must put a comma before a connector in a compound sentence.

NOTE: Sometimes *but* is not a connector. In these cases, it is a preposition that means the same as the word *except*. Consider these examples:

<u>We</u> <u>visited</u> all of the countries in South America *but* Chile and Argentina.
SUBJ.   VERB

<u>All</u> of the new cars but this one <u>are</u> luxury cars.
SUBJ.   VERB

These two sentences are simple sentences. There is only one subject-verb relationship in each sentence.

Activity 12   **Compound Sentence Review**

Read the following sentences. Some are compound sentences and some are simple. First, identify the type of sentence as S (simple) or C (compound). Then if the sentence is compound, insert a comma where it is necessary. The first three have been done for you.

1. _____S_____ The girls practiced every day.

2. _____S_____ They didn't win the tennis tournament.

3. _____C_____ The girls practiced every day, but they didn't win the tennis tournament.

4. _____ The committee members made a decision but the manager didn't like it.

5. _____ Neal worked with his father at the shoe store for almost twenty years.

6. _____ We went to Canada but we didn't visit Toronto.

7. _____ With the recent increase in crime in that area of the city, the local residents there are worried about their safety.

8. _____ Summer is a good time to practice outdoor sports but winter is not.

9. _____ All of the workers but Marian arrived at yesterday's income tax meeting on time.

10. _____ Saudi Arabia and Iraq import equipment, cars, food, and medicine.

11. _____ The chairs in the living room are made of pine but the chairs in my office are made of oak.

12. _____ All of the chairs in the kitchen but this one are made of maple.

| **Activity 13** | **Writing Compound Sentences** |

Read these charts. They give information about two brothers.

Name:	Andrew Bright		Name:	Ian Bright
Born:	January 14, 1915		Born:	May 1, 1920
Died:	March 23, 1985		Died:	September 12, 1992
Home City:	Washington, DC		Home City:	Chicago, Illinois
Education:	High school		Education:	Bachelor's degree
Work:	Firefighter		Work:	High school math teacher
Family:	Wife and five children		Family:	single
Hobbies:	singing		Hobbies:	Playing baseball

Now read the incorrect statements below about the brothers. Then write a compound sentence with but. *Use the information in the charts. The first one has been done for you.*

1. They were born on the same day.

   Andrew was born on January 14, but Ian was born on May 1.

2. The brothers were born in the same year.

   _____

3. They both sang as a hobby.

   _____

4. Both brothers were married.

   _____

5. They lived in the same city.

   _____

6. They had the same level of education.

   _____

7. Both men had the same kind of job.

   _____

8. They died on the same date.

   _____

Activity 14   **Interviewing Your Classmates**

Circulate around the classroom and ask different classmates the following questions. Write down the answers. When you have finished, complete the sentences using information about yourself and the information you received from your classmates. The first one has been done for you.

1. Where are you from? _(José is from Peru.)_ _____ I am from Kuwait, _____

   but _José is from Peru._ _____

2. What did you eat last night for dinner? _____ (I ate _____) _____

   but _____

3. Where was your last vacation? _____ (My last vacation was in _____) ___

   but _____

4. Why did you come to this school? _____ (I came to this school _____) ___

   but _____

5. What country do you want to visit? _____ (I want to visit _____) _____

   but _____

Editing

Activity 15   Editing: Grammar and Sentence Review

Read the following paragraph. Find and correct the 14 errors. If you need some help locating the errors, look at the numbers in parentheses on the left. This number tells you how many errors are in each line. The first one has been done for you.

Paragraph 45

Muhammad Ibn Batuta

(3) Ibn Batuta a famous moroccan traveler. He live
                  ^was

in Morocco in the fourteenth century. When he

(1) was a man young, he made a religious trip to

(1) Mecca. However, Ibn Batuta loves to see new

places so much that he continued to travel. This

(2) was no his original plan but he continued on his

(1) journey. He had many adventures during her

(1) travels and he met many interesting people. After

(1) he returned home, he did not forgot about his

(1) journey. He wrote a book about his travels. this

(1) book now gives us a lot of information important

(1) about life in the fourteenth century. Also gives us

more information about this interesting and

(1) important man

Activity 16   **Original Writing Practice**

Reread the paragraph about Lao-Tzu on page 81 and your answers in Activity 3 on page 82.
You will use this kind of information to write in the past tense about an important person.

Think of an important person. Then follow these steps for writing and use the checklist below.
Put a check (✓) next to each step as you complete it. Remember to write in the past tense. You
may want to review What Is a Paragraph? in Unit 2 on page 34.

Step 1 _____ In your first sentence, tell the name of the person and why that person was important.

Step 2 _____ In your next sentence, write where the person was born.

Step 3 _____ In the next sentence, tell about the person's job.

Step 4 _____ In the next three or four sentences, tell a short story about the person.

Step 5 _____ Try to use the word *but* in one of the sentences in Step 4. Remember to use a comma!

Step 6 _____ Use a *negative verb* in one of the sentences in Step 4.

Step 7 _____ In the next sentence, write why you chose this person.

Step 8 _____ In the final sentence, ask a question about this person.

Checklist

✔1. ❑ Make sure every sentence has a subject and a verb.

✔2. ❑ Make sure the verbs are the correct form of the past tense.

✔3. ❑ Make sure every sentence begins with a capital letter.

✔4. ❑ Make sure that all the proper nouns (names, cities, countries, etc.) are capitalized.

✔5. ❑ Make sure every sentence ends with the correct punctuation.

✔6. ❑ Create a title for your paragraph.

Activity 17	Peer Editing

Choose someone that you work well with. Exchange papers from Activity 16 with that student. Read your partner's paragraph. Use Peer Editing Sheet 4 on page 225 to help you talk about your partner's work.

Activity 18	Journal Writing

Here are ten ideas for journal writing. Choose one or more of them to write about. Follow your teacher's directions. (We recommend that you skip a line after each line that you write. This gives your teacher a place to write comments.)

1. Describe a pet you had in the past. What was the pet's name? What kind of animal was it? How long did you have this pet? Why did you like this pet? (*Or:* Why did you dislike this pet?)

2. Describe a home you lived in when you were a child. How big was the house? What color was the house? Where was the house? Did you like the house? What was your favorite room in the house?

3. Write about a movie you saw or a book you read. Did you like it? Who was your favorite character? What was the story about? Did the author have a message for the readers of this book?

4. Write about what you did last weekend. Where did you go? Who did you go with? Did you enjoy it?

5. Write about a person you used to know. Who was this person? Where did you meet this person? What was special about this person?

6. Write about an important event in your life. How old were you? What happened? Why is this event important to you?

7. Describe a holiday that you and your family spent together. What was the occasion? Which family members were there? What did you do?

8. Write about something embarrassing that happened to you. How old were you? What happened? Why were you embarrassed? Who saw this happen? How did you feel afterwards?

9. Write about a day you spent outdoors. What did you do? Where did you go? Who did you go with? What specific activities did you do? How was the weather?

10. Describe a vacation you took. Where did you go? What did you do? Who went on this vacation with you? How old were you when you went on this trip? Did you like this vacation?

EXTRA WRITING

Unit 5

Describing Actions

GOAL: To learn how to write in the present progressive tense

GRAMMAR AND SENTENCE STRUCTURE: Present progressive tense; adverbs of manner

SENTENCE DEVELOPMENT: Compound sentences with *and*; compound sentences with *so*

USING THE PRESENT PROGRESSIVE

When good writers write about actions that are happening at the moment, they often use the present progressive tense.

GRAMMAR AND SENTENCE STRUCTURE:
Present Progressive Tense for Current Actions

The present progressive tense (*be* + verb + *ing*) is often used to describe actions that are happening right now. Review the chart below before beginning the activities in this unit. (See Appendix 4 for spelling rules of verbs ending in *-ing*.)

Present Progressive Tense

I	**am eating**	we	**are eating**
you	**are eating**	you (plural)	**are eating**
he / she / it	**is eating**	they	**are eating**

I	**am walk_ing_**	we	**are walk_ing_**
you	**are walk_ing_**	you (plural)	**are walk_ing_**
he / she / it	**is walk_ing_**	they	**are walk_ing_**

Careful! Some verbs in English do *not* usually take the progressive tense because they are not action verbs. Here are some common stative, or non-action, verbs: *be, have, see, love, believe, own, want.* (See Appendix 5 for more information.)

| **Activity 1** | **Identifying Present Progressive Tense** |

Read the following paragraph about a Sunday afternoon at the zoo. Underline all the present progressive verbs. There are 16.

Paragraph 46

EXAMPLE PARAGRAPH

A Day Trip for the Johnson Family

The Johnson family lives in Chicago. It is a large family, with Mr. and Mrs. Johnson, their two sons Keith and Kevin, and their daughter Rosie. Today is a special day for the Johnsons. They are visiting the Chicago Zoo. Mr. Johnson and Rosie love monkeys, so they are walking to the monkey **exhibit**. They are watching the chimpanzees and orang-utans. The chimps are playing with each other, and some of them are swinging from ropes. The monkeys look like they are having a good time. One orangutan is looking at the **crowd** of people. The other orangutan is eating a banana. At the other end of the zoo, the rest of the Johnson family is walking to the lion exhibit. Keith and Kevin are talking about how beautiful the male lion is. This lion is walking around. It is **yawning**. Mrs. Johnson is talking to her sons. She is telling a story about a **safari** that she took when she was younger. Keith and Kevin are listening to their mother's story, and they are asking Mrs. Johnson to take them on a safari.

exhibit: display, performance   **yawning:** opening its mouth to show sleepiness or hunger
crowd: large group   **safari:** a trip in the jungle, often to see wild animals

| **Activity 2** | **Writing from Picture Prompts** |

Study the picture of Bruce and his friends. Then read the paragraph. Fill in the missing verbs and sentence based on what you see in the picture.

Paragraph 47

A University Student's Room

    Tomorrow is a big day for Bruce. His mother is coming to visit him for the first time at college. Bruce is very excited, but he is also worried. His dorm room is a mess. This is why he called all his friends to come help him. His good friend Lina (**1.**) _____ the floor because the carpet is very dirty. Bruce's friend Joe (**2.**) _____

_____ some of Bruce's clothes to the laundry. At the same time, Bruce's roommate Paul (**3.**) _____ all of the empty pizza boxes and soda cans. Bruce

(**4.**) _____ . Bruce feels very

lucky to have such good friends, and he is sure that the room will be ready for his mother's visit.

Activity 3	Writing from Picture Prompts

Study the picture of the soccer game. Read the prompts that are connected to each action.
Complete the sentences below using the present progressive tense.

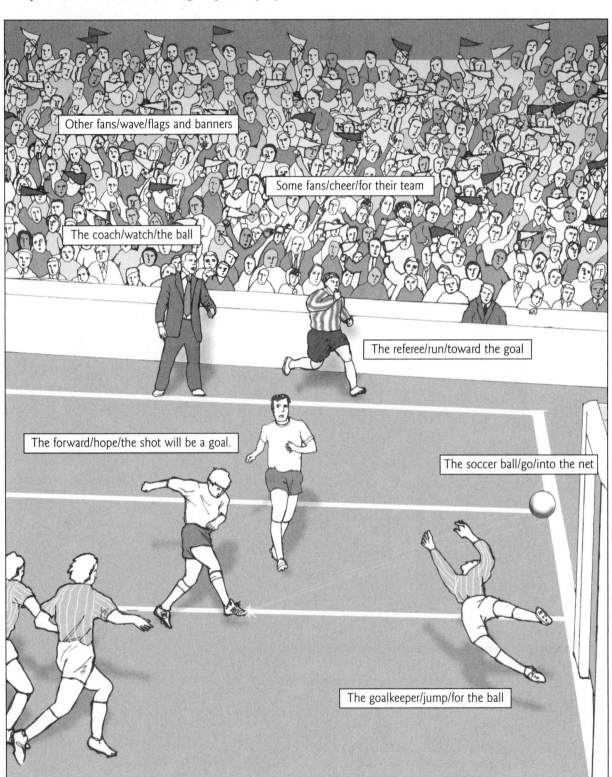

Other fans/wave/flags and banners

Some fans/cheer/for their team

The coach/watch/the ball

The referee/run/toward the goal

The forward/hope/the shot will be a goal.

The soccer ball/go/into the net

The goalkeeper/jump/for the ball

1. The soccer ball _____ .

2. The goalkeeper _____ .

3. The coach _____ .

4. The referee _____ .

5. The forward _____ .

6. Some fans _____ .

7. Other fans _____ .

When you complete the sentences, compare them to a classmate's sentences.

Activity 4   **Writing a Paragraph**

Rewrite the sentences in paragraph form. Try to use your imagination and add some extra information and adjectives about this game.

    The soccer game between Juventus and Lazio is very exciting. Many things are happening right now!

_____

_____

_____

_____

_____

_____

_____

_____

_____

USING THE CONNECTOR *AND*

In Unit 4, you practiced using the connector *but* to make compound sentences. In the following activities, you will practice another common connector—*and*.

Compound Sentences with *And*

Good writers often use the connector *and* to join words and ideas. Here are some common examples.

1. ***And* is used to join two (or more) words that are in the same grammar category (or group).**

   Example A: In the following sentence, *and* joins two <u>nouns</u> and makes the subject of the sentence plural.

   > Bobby *and* Jenny go to Oak Ridge Elementary School.

   This sentence means:

   > Bobby goes to Oak Ridge Elementary School.
   >
   > Jenny goes to Oak Ridge Elementary School.

   Example B: In the following sentence, *and* joins two <u>nouns</u> and makes the object of the sentence plural.

   > My sister loves pizza *and* spaghetti.

   This sentence means:

   > My sister loves pizza.
   >
   > My sister loves spaghetti.

   Example C: In the following sentence, *and* joins two <u>verbs</u> in a sentence.

   > Ricardo works *and* studies at the university.

   This sentence means:

   > Ricardo works at the university.
   >
   > Ricardo studies at the university.

   Example D: In the following sentence, *and* joins two <u>adjectives</u> in a sentence.

   > The weather was hot *and* muggy.

   This sentence means:

   > The weather was hot.
   >
   > The weather was muggy.

2. **The connector *and* is also used to form compound sentences.** Remember from Unit 3 that a compound sentence is two sentences joined by a comma and a connecting word. A compound sentence has two subjects and two verbs.

Example A:

Irene works at the mall, *and* her brother visits her store every day.

This sentence means:

Irene works at the mall.

Irene's brother visits her store every day.

NOTE: When you join these two sentences, you don't repeat *Irene* after the connector. You use the possessive adjective *her*.

Example B:

Joanna is washing the car, *and* her mother is cooking dinner.

This sentence means:

Joanna is washing the car.

Joanna's mother is cooking dinner.

Activity 5 | **Compound Sentence Practice**

Connect the two simple sentences into a compound sentence by using the connector and. *Remember to put a comma (,) before* and. *The first one has been done for you.*

1. John is watching a movie. Ann is eating popcorn.

   John is watching a movie, and Ann is eating popcorn.

2. Oranges contain a lot of vitamin C. Milk has a large amount of vitamin D.

   _____

3. Bolivia is a landlocked country in South America. Switzerland is a landlocked country in Europe.

   _____

4. Those pants are the perfect color for you. They are on sale.

   _____

5. I am planting marigold seeds. I hope they will grow quickly.

   _____

Activity 6	Working with the Connector *And*

Read the paragraph and complete the sentence analysis that follows.

Paragraph 48

Jobs for the Future

EXAMPLE PARAGRAPH

Dharma and Greta are studying engineering at the University of Florida. Dharma lives in a dormitory, and Greta is her roommate. They are going to graduate at the end of the year. Both Dharma and Greta want to get good jobs in the private sector when they graduate. Dharma hopes to work for Motorola, and Greta wants to get a job with Florida Power & Light Company.

Now read each sentence below. Rewrite the information using two sentences instead of one. The first one has been done for you.

1. Dharma and Greta are studying engineering at the University of Florida.

   Meaning: _Dharma is studying engineering at the University of Florida._

   Greta is studying engineering at the University of Florida.

2. Dharma lives in a dormitory, and Greta is her roommate.

   Meaning: _____

   _____

3. Dharma and Greta are going to graduate at the end of the year.

   Meaning: _____

   _____

4. Both Dharma and Greta want to get good jobs in the private sector when they graduate.

   Meaning: _____

   _____

5. Dharma hopes to work for Motorola, and Greta wants to get a job with Florida Power & Light Company.

   Meaning: _____

   _____

USING THE CONNECTOR *SO*

So is another connector that good writers use in compound sentences. This connector connects a cause and a result.

Compound Sentences with *So*

The connector *so* shows a result. The first subject and verb gives the "cause" and the second subject and verb gives the "result."

CAUSE   RESULT
I was hungry, <u>so</u> I ate a sandwich.

CAUSE   RESULT
Leslie has a big exam tomorrow, <u>so</u> she is studying at the library.

CAUSE   RESULT
The children had a long day, <u>so</u> they are taking a nap now.

NOTE: Another word for a subject and verb is **clause**. In each example there are two clauses. These sentences are compound. Remember to use a comma before *so* when it means cause and result.

| Activity 7 | Combining Sentences with *So* |

Read the two sentences. Write C (for cause) or R (for result) on the line to show what kind of sentence each is. Then combine them into a compound sentence. Put the cause first, then the connector so, *and then the result. Be sure to put a comma before* so *and add a period at the end of the sentence. The first one has been done for you.*

(Note: Sometimes you will need to change nouns to pronouns—for example, the boy ➔ *him or the car* ➔ *it.)*

1a. ___C___ I was thirsty.

  b. ___R___ I drank three glasses of water.

  I was thirsty, so I drank three glasses of water.

2a. _____ We didn't play tennis.

  b. _____ It rained really hard.

3a. _____ We took the cat to the vet.

b. _____ The cat was very sick.

_____

4a. _____ The audience loved the show.

b. _____ They applauded wildly.

_____

5a. _____ Jonathan didn't feel well.

b. _____ Jonathan didn't go to the party.

_____

6a. _____ I didn't buy the record.

b. _____ The record was very expensive.

_____

7a. _____ The plane didn't leave on time.

b. _____ We arrived at our destination late.

_____

8a. _____ She forgot to set her alarm clock.

b. _____ She woke up late.

_____

Activity 8   **Scenarios: Writing Compound Sentences with *So* and the Present Progressive**

Study the following pictures. Write what you think is happening based on what you see. Be sure to use the connector so *and the present progressive in your compound sentences. The first one has been done for you.*

1. The woman wants to lose weight, so she is exercising.

2. _____

3. _____

_____

4. _____

_____

5. _____

_____

6. _____

_____

Activity 9   Compound Sentence Review

Read the following sentences. Some of the sentences are compound sentences and some are simple. First, identify the type of sentence as S (simple) or C (compound). Then, if the sentence is compound, insert a comma where necessary. The first two have been done for you.

1. ___S___ My brother and I went hiking and fishing last weekend.

2. ___C___ The motorcycle is in the garage, and the car is in the driveway.

3. _____ Harry and Darlene went to the picnic yesterday and the party last night.

4. _____ I don't know the answer to the question so I will ask the teacher.

5. _____ How many times have you visited Europe and Asia?

6. _____ There are many great places to visit in this city so you can't see them all in one day.

7. _____ The main agricultural product from the countries in that area of central Asia is rice.

8. _____ Nouns are words like *cat*, *dog*, and *honesty* and verbs are action words such as *eat*, *drink*, and *run*.

9. _____ Lisana works for IBM but she doesn't have a computer engineering degree.

10. _____ Where did you get those beautiful earrings and rings?

11. _____ The capital of Sudan is Khartoum and it is the most populated city in the country.

12. _____ She missed her plane so she didn't get home on time.

WRITER'S NOTE: Use Sentence Variety

Many students who are studying English write short sentences. These sentences usually follow the same pattern: simple subject + simple verb. Good writers do not repeat the same sentence patterns too often. They write some short sentences and some longer sentences. Vary your writing with both simple and compound sentences. Use connectors to show that you can write more advanced sentences in English.

ADVERBS

Adverbs are another interesting word group in English. There are several kinds of adverbs in English. Most of them describe verbs.

GRAMMAR AND SENTENCE STRUCTURE:
Common Adverbs of Manner

In Unit 2 you studied adjectives. These are words that describe nouns.

> Did you see the <u>beautiful</u> baby? The baby is <u>beautiful</u>.

In these sentences, the adjective *beautiful* describes the baby.

Adverbs also describe, but adverbs usually describe verbs.

> Kerry picked up the puppy <u>carefully</u>.
> My sister studies <u>hard</u>.

In these examples, the adverbs describe how the action is done. *How* shows manner.

> *How* did Kerry pick up the puppy? <u>Carefully</u>.
> *How* does my sister study? <u>Hard</u>.

NOTE: Adverbs of manner usually end in *-ly* and usually follow the verb.

Here is a list of some common adverbs of manner that describe actions:

> quickly   easily   nervously   carefully   happily   slowly
> suddenly   silently   correctly   fast*   hard*   well*

* These adverbs do *not* use the *-ly* form.

Activity 10   **Practice with Adverbs**

Read each sentence. In the blank, write an adverb that describes the action of the verb (underlined). You may choose from the list of common adverbs of manner or use your own adverbs.

1. Joann <u>is studying</u> _____ in the library.

2. She <u>jumped</u> on the bus _____ because it was raining.

3. Mary Ann <u>spoke</u> _____ at the conference.

4. David <u>is doing</u> _____ in this class. He never studies!

5. Norma <u>cried</u> _____ during the movie.

| Activity 11 | Writing What You See: Describing Actions |

Write a paragraph based on observation. Choose a place from which to observe people, for example, a park, a mall, or a cafeteria. You may also use a show on television or an illustration in a magazine. Be sure to choose something that has several people who are doing different actions. Use the following questions to help you write a paragraph. The paragraph has been started for you.

- Look at the people. What are they doing?
- Write about an object. What is happening with it?
- Remember to use the connectors *and* and *so* if possible.

There is a lot of action happening right now.

_____

_____

_____

_____

_____

_____

_____

_____

_____

_____

_____

Editing

| Activity 12 | Editing: Grammar and Sentence Review |

Read the following paragraph. There are ten mistakes in the paragraph: two (2) mistakes with compound sentences, two (2) mistakes with adverbs, two (2) mistakes with verbs, two (2) mistakes with adjectives, and two (2) mistakes with capitalization. Find and correct the errors. The first one has been done for you.

Paragraph 49

The Squirrel

                                    is
A small brown squirrel climbing a tree. He looks like a young squirrel. His tail is twitching
                          ∧

nervously and his nose is moving quick. I think he is looking for food. Now the squirrel brown

is on a long tree branch. He wants to jump to another tree. The squirrel hears something so he

looks down. he is coming down from the tree green. Someone dropped a few pieces of

chocolate chip cookie. These pieces lying on the grass. the squirrel is walking toward the food,

and he is inspecting it. He is putting it in his mouth. His tail is moving rapid. The little brown

squirrel is now eating happily.

Activity 13 | **Original Writing Practice**

Imagine that you are a TV news reporter. Right now you are at the location of some problem. Describe what is happening around you. Use your imagination!

Now follow these steps for writing and use the checklist below. Put a check (✓) next to each step as you complete it. You may want to review What Is a Paragraph? *in Unit 2 on page 34.*

Step 1 _____ In your first sentence, tell where you are and what you are watch-ing.

Step 2 _____ In your next sentence, describe the person, people, or things you see. Use adjectives to give a clear idea to your reader.

Step 3 _____ In the next two to four sentences, describe what the people are doing.

Step 4 _____ Use one or two adverbs in the sentences in Step 3. Remember to place them correctly (usually after the verb).

Step 5 _____ Use *and* or *so* in one of the sentences. Remember to use a comma to separate the two clauses.

Step 6 _____ In the next sentence, write what you think the people are think-ing at this moment.

Step 7 _____ In the final sentence, write your opinion about these people.

Checklist

✔1. ❏ Make sure every sentence has a subject and a verb.

✔2. ❏ Be sure that the compound sentences have two subjects and verbs, or clauses.

✔3. ❏ Make sure you use the present progressive verbs correctly.

✔4. ❏ Make sure every sentence begins with a capital letter.

✔5. ❏ Make sure every sentence ends with the correct punctuation.

✔6. ❏ Create a title for your paragraph.

Activity 14   Peer Editing

Choose someone that you work well with. Exchange papers from Activity 13 with that student. Read your partner's paragraph. Use Peer Editing Sheet 5 on page 227 to help you talk about your partner's work.

Activity 15   Journal Writing

Here are ten ideas for journal writing. Choose one or more of them to write about. Follow your teacher's directions. (We recommend that you skip a line after each line that you write. This gives your teacher a place to write comments.)

1. Watch several minutes of a television program. Describe what is happening in the show.

2. Describe how your life is now. Include your studies, your living arrangements, and your free time.

3. Imagine that you are a private investigator. Imagine a specific character or person. Write down everything that person did for five minutes.

4. Find a picture in a magazine. Choose a picture of many people who are doing different things. Write a paragraph that describes what each person is doing.

5. Imagine that you are visiting the zoo. What are the animals doing? Write a paragraph that tells what at least five different kinds of animals are doing. Use the connectors *and*, *but*, or *so* to combine short sentences into longer sentences.

EXTRA WRITING

6. Imagine that you are in a large city like Chicago, Illinois, or Toronto, Canada. Walk around the city and write down the things that you see. What is happening in this large city?

7. Imagine that you are walking down the street, and you see your favorite movie star walk into a café. Follow this person. What is he/she doing?

8. Write a letter to your friend explaining what you are doing in this class. Tell about the assignments that you have and the writing skills that you are practicing.

9. If you have a pet, watch it closely for ten minutes. What is it doing? Where is it going? Is it playing? Jumping? Making noise?

10. Imagine that you are a news reporter for a movie magazine. You are at the Academy Awards presentation. What are the people doing? Name some of the famous actors. (This word means male and female actors.) What are they doing? What are they wearing? What are they saying to their friends? What are they wondering?

EXTRA WRITING

Unit 6

Writing About the Future

GOAL: To learn how to write in the future tense

GRAMMAR AND SENTENCE STRUCTURE: *Be going to* for future: statements, questions, negatives; time words to show the future; articles; using commas in a list

SENTENCE DEVELOPMENT: Complex sentences; answering questions with *because*

TALKING ABOUT THE FUTURE

There are many ways to talk about events that will happen in the future. One way is to use *be going to*. You can use *be going to* when you talk about future plans or when you want to make predictions—or guesses—about the future.

GRAMMAR AND SENTENCE STRUCTURE:
Be Going To: Statements and Questions

Be going to is easy to form. Just put *be* + *going to* in front of the base form of the verb.

118

Be Going To: Statements

I	**am going to study**	we	**are going to study**
you	**are going to study**	you (plural)	**are going to study**
he / she / it	**is going to study**	they	**are going to study**

Study these examples.

Incorrect: We going to go to the store in a few minutes.

Correct: We are going to go to the store in a few minutes.

Incorrect: I am going to a sandwich for lunch.

Correct: I am going to buy a sandwich for lunch.

Incorrect: According to the radio report, the weather going to be severe tonight.

Correct: According to the radio report, the weather is going to be severe tonight.

Be Going To: Questions

Verb *fly*

Am I going to fly . . . ?   **Are we going to fly** . . . ?

Are you going to fly . . . ?   **Are you** (plural) **going to fly** . . . ?

Is he / she / it **going to fly** . . . ?   **Are they going to fly** . . . ?

Study these examples.

Incorrect: Jim and Dave are going to buy a new car?

Correct: Are Jim and Dave going to buy a new car?

Incorrect: They going to see a movie this afternoon?

Correct: Are they going to see a movie this afternoon?

Incorrect: Did you going to visit your parents in December?

Correct: Are you going to visit your parents in December?

Activity I   Making Predictions

Look at each picture. Make a prediction about what will happen. Use the correct form of be going to. *Write complete sentences.*

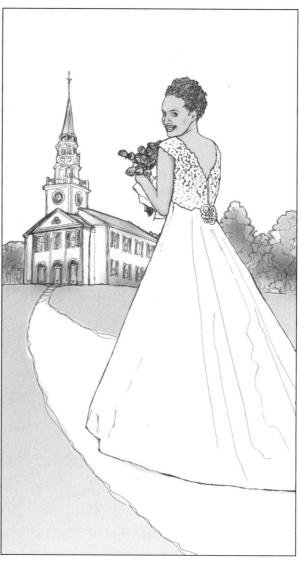

1. _____   2. _____

   _____   _____

   _____   _____

   _____   _____

3. _____

_____

4. _____

_____

5. _____

_____

_____

_____

_____

6. _____

_____

_____

_____

_____

WRITER'S NOTE: Don't Use *Gonna* in Writing

Speakers of English often pronounce *going to* as *gonna*. However, do not use *gonna* in writing. You must write out the words completely.

Incorrect writing:	I'm gonna buy a new shirt.
Correct writing:	I'm going to buy a new shirt.

Activity 2   Writing About Future Plans

Look at Michael's schedule for next week. Answer the questions using complete sentences. The first one has been done for you.

Sunday	Monday	Tuesday	Wednesday	Thursday	Friday	Saturday
Meet Mom & Dad for lunch	Meeting with Mr. Green	Take dog to the veterinarian	Business report due to Ms. Simms	Buy groceries	Dinner with Andrea	Soccer game 6pm

1. What is Michael going to do on Sunday?

   Michael is going to meet his mom and dad for lunch on Sunday.

2. Who is Michael going to meet on Monday?

   _____

3. When is he going to have dinner with Andrea?

   _____

4. Where is he going to take his pet?

   _____

5. What is he going to do on Thursday?

   _____

6. When is he going to play soccer?

   _____

7. What is he going to give to Ms. Simms on Wednesday?

   _____

| Activity 3 | Practicing with Paragraphs |

Review the sentences you wrote about Michael's schedule in Activity 2. Put them in correct time order, starting with Sunday. Write the sentences in paragraph form below. The beginning and the end of the paragraph have been done for you.

Michael's Busy Schedule

Michael is going to be a very busy man next week! He is going to meet his mom and dad for lunch

on Sunday.

_____

_____

_____

_____

_____

_____

_____

_____

_____

Finally, he is going to play soccer at six o'clock on Saturday. Michael is the busiest man I know!

USING TIME WORDS

Good writers include *time words* and *time phrases* in their writing. Time words and phrases give important information about *when* something happens.

GRAMMAR AND SENTENCE STRUCTURE:
Time Words and Phrases

Study this list of time words. (They are adverbs. Remember that adverbs are words that modify verbs.) Do you know the meanings of all of them?

first	tomorrow	in a minute	next week
next	next Saturday	later	next year
finally	next January	then	next time
after that	before that		

Time words usually occur at the beginning or the end of a sentence. However, they can sometimes occur in the middle of a sentence. Look at these examples of time words and phrases at the beginning and at the end of sentences.

We are going to go to the movies <u>on Saturday</u>.

<u>On Saturday</u>, we are going to go to the movies.

Angela is going to study in France <u>next year</u>.

<u>Next year</u> Angela is going to study in France.

The airline will produce a new kind of jet <u>in the next few months</u>.

<u>In the next few months</u>, the airline will produce a new kind of jet.

We are going to paint the kitchen <u>first</u>.

<u>First</u>, we are going to paint the kitchen.

Notice that a comma immediately follows the time words and phrases at the beginning of the sentence.

Activity 4   Practicing with Time Words

Fill in the blanks with these time words and phrases: next, first, after that, Tuesday, finally.

Paragraph 50

A Week to Forget

Last week was a really bad week for me. (**1.**) _____ , I was sick on Monday.

On (**2.**) _____ , I overslept and was late for work. My boss was really angry at

me. Wednesday was especially bad. I made a huge mistake with the amount of a check. The (**3.**)

_____ day I was sick again. (**4.**) _____ , two things happened on

Friday. My car didn't start that morning, so I took a taxi to work. (5.) _____ , I

forgot to call my mother on her birthday. She didn't get angry, but I think she was hurt. What

a horrible week!

| Activity 5 | Responding to a Reading Passage |

Read the paragraph and underline the ten future tense verbs. (Hint: Three of them might be difficult to find.) Then answer the questions that follow.

Paragraph 51

Carmen's Fifteenth Birthday

Next week Carmen Viera is going to be 15 years old. Her family has plans for a special celebration for her. On her birthday, Carmen is going to wear a beautiful white **gown**. First, she is going to go to church with her family and friends. After church is over, they are going to go to a beautiful **ballroom**. Then they are going to have a party called a *quince*. When Carmen arrives, she is going to perform some formal dances with her friends. After that, everyone is going to dance, eat, and celebrate. Carmen can **hardly** wait. She is never going to forget such a special day.

gown: a long, formal dress
ballroom: a large room where formal parties are held

quince: the Spanish word for fifteen; a traditional Latin birthday party that celebrates when a girl becomes a woman
hardly: with difficulty

1. How old is Carmen going to be next week?

   _____

2. What is Carmen going to wear on her birthday?

   _____

3. What is the first thing she is going to do on her birthday?

   _____

4. Where is her *quince* party going to be held?

_____

5. What are Carmen and her friends going to do at the party?

_____

BE GOING TO WITH NEGATIVES

You know how to use *be + going to* to talk about events that will happen in the future. You learned how to make affirmative statements and how to ask questions about the future. It is also important to know how to talk about things that are not going to happen in the future.

GRAMMAR AND SENTENCE STRUCTURE:
Be Going To: Negative

To make *be going to* negative, write the word *not* between the *be* verb and *going*.

Examples:

The price of gasoline is <u>not</u> going to get higher.

We are <u>not</u> going to bed now.

I am <u>not</u> going to plant a garden this year.

Study this chart of *be going to* with the negative *not*.

I	**am <u>not</u> going to study**	we	**are <u>not</u> going to study**
you	**are <u>not</u> going to study**	you (plural)	**are <u>not</u> going to study**
he / she / it	**is <u>not</u> going to study**	they	**are <u>not</u> going to study**

NOTE: You can make contractions with these negative verbs.

are not = aren't   is not = isn't

Here are some examples:

Incorrect: I am going to not talk.

Correct: I am (I'm) not going to talk.

Incorrect: Jane not going to sing on Sunday.

Correct: Jane is not (isn't) going to sing on Sunday.

Incorrect: Brett and Erica no going to play soccer.

Correct: Brett and Erica are not (aren't) going to play soccer.

| Activity 6 | Writing Original Sentences |

Think of something important or special that you are going to do in the future. Answer these questions.

1. What is one important thing that you are going to do in your life?

   _____

   _____

2. How long is it going to take to do it?

   _____

3. What are you are going to do to accomplish this thing? (Write at least three things.)

   _____

   _____

   _____

   _____

   _____

   _____

4. How are you going to feel when you accomplish this thing? Why?

   _____

   _____

COMPLEX SENTENCES

In Unit 5, you learned that sentence variety is important. Good writers write both simple and compound sentences. There is another way to add variety to your sentence writing. You can put two clauses (each with a subject and verb) together when one of them begins with a different kind of connecting word.

Sentence Variety: Complex Sentences

One way to combine two sentences into one is to use a connecting word that is part of the sentence. Some of these connecting words are *after*, *before*, *because*, *if*, *although*, *since*, and *when*. Unlike the connectors in compound sentences (*and*, *but*, *so*), the connecting words in complex sentences are a necessary part of one of the sentences (clauses). This type of sentence is called a complex sentence. Look at these examples:

Compound sentence: Joe played tennis, and Vicky watched TV.

This sentence has three parts: one sentence + one sentence joined by *and*.

Joe played tennis / and / Vicky watched T.V.

Complex sentence: Joe played tennis after Vicky watched TV.

This sentence has two parts: one simple sentence + one sentence that begins with the connecting word *after*.

Joe played tennis / after Vicky watched TV.

The word *after* is not a part by itself. This word is part of the idea of *when* Vicky watched TV. The group of words with the connecting word must always be connected to another sentence. Otherwise, it is a *fragment*. (See Unit 1, pages 17–18, for information on fragments.)

Here are a few more examples of complex sentences.

My mom is going to make dinner <u>when</u> my dad gets home.

Alana is going to get a full-time job <u>after</u> she graduates.

<u>As soon as</u> we get paid, we are going to buy some new clothes.

<u>Because</u> it is cold outside, they are going to wear jackets.

Commas in Complex Sentences

When a complex sentence begins with a clause that contains a connecting word, put a comma at the end of the clause.

	CONNECTING WORD CLAUSE
No comma:	She called up her friend <u>after she ate dinner</u>.

	CONNECTING WORD CLAUSE
Comma:	<u>After she ate dinner</u>, she called up her friend.

WRITER'S NOTE: Verbs in Complex Sentences

Here is a rule for writing complex sentences about the *future*: Use the *present tense* in the clause with the time word. Use the *future tense* in the other clause. Do not use future tense in both clauses.

Example:

When the rain stops, I'm going to rake the leaves.

Activity 7   **Identifying Sentence Types**

Read the following sentences. Some of the sentences are simple, some are compound, and some are complex. First, identify the type of sentence as S (simple), CD (compound), or CX (complex). Then if the sentence is compound or complex, insert a comma if necessary. The first three have been done for you.

1. __S__   I'm going to go scuba diving next weekend.

2. __CD__   My father is going to retire next year, but my mother is going to continue working.

3. __CX__   After he came home from the beach, Gerardo took a shower.

4. _____   Irene is going to call you when she gets home from work.

5. _____   We're going to go to the mall and the beach next Sunday.

6. _____   Wilma is going to go to college next year but her brother is going to get a job.

7. _____   When the game is over we're going to Harvey's Grill.

8. _____   How often do you work out at the gym?

9. _____   Leslie and Gertrude are sisters but they don't get along very well.

10. _____   Billy and his friends went to the hockey game and cheered for their team.

11. _____   If the pilot gets sick during a flight the copilot takes over.

12. _____   The copilot plays an important role in the success of a flight.

Activity 8	Writing Complex Sentences in the Future

Answer the following questions. Use time words in your answer. If the question includes time words, write a complex sentence for your answer. In sentences that do not include time words, add them. You can use the time words in the Grammar and Sentence Structure on page 125.

1. What are you going to do after you graduate?

   After I graduate, I am going to look for a job.

2. What are you going to do as soon as you finish this exercise?

3. What are you not going to do before you go to bed tonight?

4. When are you going to do your homework?

5. When are you going to eat dinner?

6. What are you going to do after you eat dinner?

ARTICLES *A, AN, THE*

A, *an,* and *the* are three of the shortest words in English, but they are also three of the most important words. These words are articles. They are very important in correct writing and speaking. In this section, you are going to learn about the uses of these three words.

GRAMMAR AND SENTENCE STRUCTURE:
Using Articles in a Sentence

Good writers always use articles in the correct places. There are many rules for using articles in English.

A/An—Indefinite Articles

Use *a/an* when you have a singular count noun and are talking about something in general. Use *a* if the next word begins with a consonant sound. Use *an* if the next word begins with a vowel sound.

> I bought <u>a</u> sweater.

> Wendy wants <u>an</u> ice cream cone.

There are some exceptions to the consonant/vowel rule. If the beginning letter *h* is silent (as in *honor*), use *an* before it. If the beginning letter *u* sounds like the word *you* (as in *university*), use *a* before it. Remember to pay attention to the *sound* of the beginning of the word, not the letter that it begins with.

Incorrect:	Meet me at the library in a hour.
Correct:	Meet me at the library in an hour.
Incorrect:	John bought an unique gift for his mother.
Correct:	John bought a unique gift for his mother.
Incorrect:	Does your last name begin with a *e* or a *n*?
Correct:	Does your last name begin with an *e* or an *n*?

The—Definite Article

The can be used with both singular and plural count and noncount* nouns. Here are some basic rules for using *the*.

1. Use *the* for the second (and subsequent) time you talk about something.

   > I bought a sweater and a coat yesterday.

   > *The* sweater is made of wool, but *the* coat is made of leather.

2. Use *the* when the speaker and the listener both know about or are familiar with the subject.

   > Are you going to <u>the bank</u> this afternoon?

* Noncount nouns are nouns that do not use a plural form: money butter homework gold honesty
Examples: Honesty is important. (not *the honesty*)
      When people discuss politics, they often disagree. (not *the politics*)
(See Appendix 7 for a list of more noncount nouns.)

3. Use *the* when the noun you are referring to is unique—there is only one.

   The sun and the Earth are both in the Milky Way galaxy.

   The Eiffel Tower is a beautiful monument.

(See Appendix 6 for a more complete list of when to use the article *the*.)

Article Use Chart

Here is a chart that will help you remember the basic rules for using articles:

When Your Meaning Is:	Article	Singular Count Nouns	Plural Count Nouns	Noncount Nouns
General	*a*	yes	no	no
General	*an*	yes	no	no
Specific	*the*	yes	yes	yes

*Count nouns are nouns that have a plural form:
   cat—cats   woman—women   child—children   house—houses

WRITER'S NOTE: Single Count Nouns and Modifiers

A singular count noun (*car, woman*) can never stand on its own in a sentence. An article (*a, an, the*), a possessive adjective (*my, your, his*), or a quantifier (*one, another, some*) *must* come before it. (See Appendix 8 for more examples of possessive adjectives. See Appendix 9 for more examples of quantifiers.) Look at the following sentences.

Incorrect:	April owns dog.
Correct:	April owns <u>a</u> dog.
Incorrect:	I am reading book.
Correct:	I am reading <u>my</u> book.
Incorrect:	Give me spoon. This one is dirty.
Correct:	Give me <u>another</u> spoon. This one is dirty. (quantifier)

Activity 9   Articles

Read the paragraph. Write a, an, *or* the *in the blanks.*

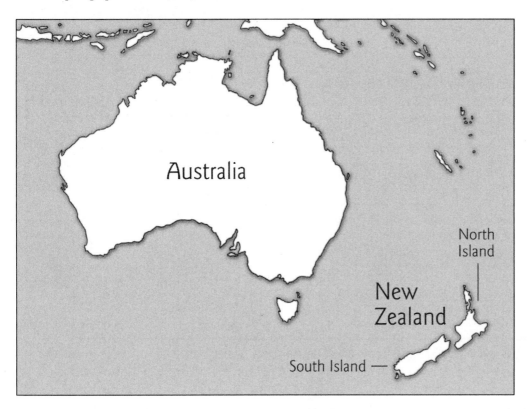

Paragraph 52

A World Traveler

Robert likes to travel a lot. Next year he is going to go on (**1.**) _____ excellent trip. (**2.**)

_____ trip is going to be to Egypt and New Zealand. He wants to meet a lot of new people

and try interesting food. While he is in Egypt, he is going to see (**3.**) _____ Great Pyramids

at Giza and (**4.**) _____ Sphinx of Cheops. He wants to take (**5.**) _____ cruise down (**6.**)

_____ Nile River, but it is probably going to be too expensive. After he visits Egypt, he is

going to fly to New Zealand to visit (**7.**) _____ cousin who lives there. His cousin's name

is Thomas. Robert and Thomas are going to hike along the coast of New Zealand for a few weeks. They want to see (**8.**) _____ tuatara. Tuataras are lizards from (**9.**) _____ ancient

reptile family. Because tuataras are nocturnal, it is going to be difficult to see them. Finally,

they are going to take (**10.**) _____ bike trip on (**11.**) _____ North Island.

Activity 10 | **Sentence Writing: Review**

Create complete sentences and questions from the prompts below. Remember to add the correct article (a, an, the) *to the sentences where necessary. Use the correct verb tense, punctuation, and capitalization. The first one has been done for you.*

1. robert / go (negative) / to / beach / tomorrow

   Robert is not going to the beach tomorrow.

2. laura's parents / visit / eiffel tower / in paris / last year

   _____

3. we / have / grammar test / next week (question)

   _____

4. weather / be / very / nice / for / picnic / last saturday

   _____

5. carol / bob / see / owl / in / tree / in their back yard / last night

   _____

6. you / go / movies / every friday night (question)

   _____

7. computer / not work / anymore

   _____

8. I / bring / apple / sandwich / for lunch yesterday

   _____

9. after nicholas / graduate last week / his sister / give him / expensive gift

   _____

10. my dad / buy / me / bike / for / my last birthday / but / I / want / puppy

   _____

QUESTIONS AND ANSWERS: STRUCTURES WITH *BECAUSE*

You have learned that one way to write complex sentences is with words such as *after*, *before*, *when*, and *if*. In this section, you are going to learn how to write complex sentences with the connector *because*.

Answering Questions with *Because*

How would you answer this question: *Why did you decide to study English?*
One popular way to answer a *why* question is to use the word *because* in the answer.

I studied English <u>because</u> I wanted to learn a second language.

I studied English <u>because</u> I want to study in an English-speaking country.

I studied English <u>because</u> I like the way it sounds.

Notice how these sentences are organized. The first part of each sentence contains part of the question. It is then followed by *because*. The word *because* is followed by the reason (answer). Each example sentence has two clauses. Remember a clause has a subject and a verb. In formal writing, a clause with *because* must be part of a complex sentence.

If your sentence has *because* and one subject and verb only, the sentence is incorrect—it is a fragment. Fragments are not correct in formal writing. Study the following sentences.

Incorrect:	We didn't go to the beach. Because it was raining. (fragment)
Correct:	We didn't go to the beach because it was raining. (complex sentence)

SENTENCE DEVELOPMENT

Incorrect:	Megan is going to the disco. Because she likes to dance. (fragment)
Correct:	Megan is going to the disco because she likes to dance. (complex sentence)

NOTE: *Because* can also be used at the beginning of a sentence. When it is, you must put a comma at the end of the clause.

Incorrect:	Because they like to exercise Steve and Ken are going to the gym.
Correct:	Because they like to exercise, Steve and Ken are going to the gym.

Activity 11   **Sentence or Fragment?**

Read each group of words. If it is a fragment, write F on the line. If it is a complete sentence, write S on the line and add correct capitalization and punctuation. The first two have been done for you.

1. ___S___ D̶ante passed the test because he studied hard.

2. ___F___ because the test has 50 questions

3. _____ because it was raining we didn't go to the beach

4. _____ because everyone had a wonderful time at the party

5. _____ she arrived late because her car broke down

6. _____ because he played poorly in the last match

7. _____ because I live in new york I go to the theater on broadway often

8. _____ because some committee members did not attend the conference

9. _____ the computers were down today because a storm knocked out power

10. _____ we are going to postpone the meeting because the managers are going to a conference

Activity 12   **Using *Because* to Answer a Question**

Answer the following questions, using because *in your answer. Write complete sentences.*
The first one has been done for you.

1. Why are you studying English?

   I am studying English because I want to enter Cornell University next year.

2. Why is soccer a popular sport?

   _____

3. Why is fast food popular in the United States?

   _____

4. Why do you like your hobby?

   _____

5. Why do some people like to drive fast?

   _____

6. Why are you using this book?

   _____

7. Why do you write letters to your family?

   _____

8. Why do some people eat breakfast in the morning?

   _____

9. Why do children learn to print before they learn cursive writing?

   _____

10. Why is hip-hop music popular?

_____

WRITER'S NOTE: Use Commas Between Words in a List

The comma (,) is one of the most important marks of punctuation in English sentences. Commas help to make the meaning of sentences clear.

Sometimes good writers write sentences that contain a list of three or more things. Here are some examples.

ITEM 1   ITEM 2   ITEM 3   ITEM 4

Jennifer visited London, Paris, Rome, and Prague. (list of nouns)

ITEM 1   ITEM 2   ITEM 3

Andrea grows pink, yellow, and white roses in her garden. (list of adjectives)

You must put a comma after each item in the list except the last one. In addition, try to keep the words the same part of speech. For example, if you have three words, all three words should be nouns (or verbs or adjectives). The point is not to mix up the kinds of words.

(See Appendix 11 for more comma rules.)

Activity 13   **Practicing Comma Rules**

For each item, combine the sentences into one sentence. Remember the comma rules that you have practiced for compound sentences, complex sentences, and lists. You may have to change or delete some words. The first one has been done for you.

1. I went to the mall. I bought a new shirt and skirt. I got a winter coat.

   I went to the mall, and I bought a new shirt, skirt, and winter coat.

2. Michael likes to play soccer. He likes to play hockey and football.

   _____

   _____

3. My friend Rick is tall. He is strong and handsome.

_____

_____

4. John wants to go to the movies. Robert and Theo want to go, too.

_____

_____

5. When I go to the beach tomorrow, I am going to bring sunglasses and a towel. I am also going to bring a cold drink and a book.

_____

_____

6. At the dance, we ate food. We danced, and we played games.

_____

_____

7. In Moscow, Candice is going to visit the Kremlin and St. Basil's Cathedral. She is going to go to Gorky Park.

_____

_____

8. Ron and Harry rode the Ferris wheel at the fair. Elizabeth rode the Ferris wheel.

_____

_____

Editing

Activity 14 | Editing: Grammar and Sentence Review

Read the following paragraph. There are ten errors in the paragraph. Find and correct them. If you need help finding the errors, look at the numbers in parentheses on the left side of the paragraph. This number tells you how many errors are on each line. The first one has been done for you.

Paragraph 51

My Winter Vacation

  My winter vacation is going to be wonderful because I am going to go to

(2) Montreal with my best friend. We going to spend two weeks there, and it
    M

(2) is going to be a wonderful time. I have the aunt who lives there, and she going to

(3) show us all the sights beautiful. I don't speak french very well so I'm a little bit

(1) nervous. After I arrive in Canada I am going to buy a lot of souvenirs for my

(2) parents brother and friends.

Activity 15   **Original Writing Practice**

Reread the paragraph on Carmen Viera in Activity 5 on page 126. Then review your answers to Activity 6 on page 128. Use the information from Activity 6 to write about an event that is going to happen to you in the future.

Then follow these steps for writing, and use the checklist. Put a check (✓) next to each step as you complete it. You may want to review What Is a Paragraph? in Unit 2 on page 34.

Step 1 _____ In your first sentence, tell who you are and what you are going to do in the future.

Step 2 _____ In the next two sentences, give more details to describe what you are going to do.

Step 3 _____ In the next four or five sentences, describe how you are going to complete this thing.

Step 4 _____ In the last sentence, tell why it is important for you to do this thing. (Use the word *because* in the final sentence.)

Step 5 _____ Try to use time words such as *after* and *as soon as* in some of your sentences in Step 3.

Step 6 _____ Try to include a list of three or more items in one of the sentences in Step 3. Remember the comma rule!

Step 7 _____ Write at least one compound and one complex sentence in your paragraph.

Checklist

✔1. ❑ Did you use *be going to* when you talked about the future?

✔2. ❑ Make sure that you use articles correctly in your sentences.

✔3. ❑ Make sure that you use commas correctly.

✔4. ❑ Make sure every sentence has a subject and a verb—no fragments!

✔5. ❑ Create a title for your paragraph.

| Activity 16 | Peer Editing |

Choose someone that you work well with. Exchange papers from Activity 15 with that student. Read your partner's paragraph. Use Peer Editing Sheet 6 on page 229 to help you talk about your partner's work.

| Activity 17 | Journal Writing |

Here are ten ideas for journal writing. Choose one or more of them to write about. Follow your teacher's directions. (We recommend that you skip a line after each line that you write. This gives your teacher a place to write comments.)

1. Write about something that you plan to do in the next two weeks. Include the people who are going to be with you, where you are going to be, and why you are going to do this.

2. Write about something that you plan to do in the next six months. Be sure to include where this activity is going to happen, who is going to be with you, and why you chose this activity.

3. Choose a current topic in the news. Read about it. Then write about what you think is going to happen and tell why.

4. Write about one of your goals. Include what the goal is, why this goal is important to you, and how long it is going to take to achieve.

5. Write about what you are going to do before you return home today. Make a list: Who are you going to be with? Are you going to do this thing for work, school, or pleasure? How long is it going to take you to complete these things?

6. Describe what your wedding is going to be like. How big is the wedding party going to be? Who is going to be there? Where is it going to happen?

7. Describe the job you want to have when you finish school. What kind of job is it? What are your responsibilities going to be in this job? Are you going to work for a company or by yourself? How much money are you going to earn in this job?

8. Write about what you plan to study (your major) in college. Why did you choose this subject? What classes are going to be easy for you, and what classes are going to be difficult? How long is it going to take you to get your degree?

9. Describe what life is going to be like in the year 2050. What new things are going to be available? How is life going to be better than it is now? How is life going to be worse than it is now?

10. Write about the future of space travel. What planets are humans going to visit? What things are going to be discovered in space?

EXTRA WRITING

Unit 7

Writing Sentences with Adjective Clauses and Place Phrases

GOAL: To learn how to write sentences with adjective clauses and place phrases

GRAMMAR AND SENTENCE STRUCTURE: Place phrases

SENTENCE DEVELOPMENT Sentences with adjective clauses

WRITING WITH ADJECTIVE CLAUSES

A paragraph usually contains several sentences. It is important that the sentences not be all one kind. If they are, your paragraph can be boring to read. You have already learned some things about sentence variety. You learned about compound sentences (Units 3–5) and complex sentences (Unit 6). In this unit, you will learn about sentences with adjective clauses.

RECOGNIZING SENTENCE VARIETY

Each paragraph below contains similar information about tennis terms. However, one of the paragraphs sounds better than the other two. Read the three paragraphs. Which one do you think is best? Why?

Paragraph 54

Tennis Terms

Example 1

Tennis has many special terms. Most people do not know what these terms mean. One special word is *love*. In tennis *love* means "nothing" or "zero." Another word is *deuce*. *Deuce* is a special term. Deuce means the score is tied at three points for each player. Another term is *volley*. A volley is a shot. Usually a player runs to the net to try to end the point. The player hits the ball before it touches the ground. *Love, deuce,* and *volley* are special words. (92 words, 12 sentences)

Example 2

Tennis has many special terms. Tennis players understand these terms. Some people do not play tennis. Most of these people do not have any idea about the meaning of these terms. *Love* has a special meaning in tennis. For example, in tennis *love* means "nothing" or "zero." Another word is *deuce*. When tennis players use this word, it means each player has three points. In other words, deuce means the score is tied at three points for each player. Another term is *volley*. A volley is a shot. The player hits this shot before the ball touches the ground. Usually a player runs to the net to try to end the point. The player hits the ball before it touches the ground. *Love, deuce,* and *volley* are special words. All tennis players certainly know these words. (152 words, 20 sentences)

Example 3

Tennis has many special terms that tennis players know. Most people who do not play tennis do not understand the meaning of these terms. For example, one special word is *love*. In tennis, *love* means "nothing" or "zero." Another word that tennis players use is *deuce*. *Deuce* is a special term that means each player has three points. In other words, deuce means the score is tied at three points for each player. Another term that is used by tennis players is *volley*. A volley is a shot that the player hits before the ball touches the ground. Usually a player runs to the net to try to end the point. The player hits the ball before it touches the ground. *Love, deuce,* and *volley* are special words that all tennis players certainly know. (145 words, 12 sentences)

EVALUATING THE PARAGRAPHS

Example 1: Many sentences are short and choppy. The information does not flow smoothly or connect well. Here are some poor sentences from Example 1:

> *Deuce* is a special term.
>
> Another term is *volley*.
>
> A volley is a shot.

Example 2: This paragraph is better. For example, this complex sentence is an improvement:

> When tennis players use this word, it means each player has three points.

However, there are still a few short, choppy sentences. Some information is repeated in different sentences. Here are some poor sentences from Example 2:

Tennis has many special terms. Tennis players understand these terms.

Another term is *volley*. A volley is a shot.

Example 3: Did you think this is the best paragraph? Well, it is. The sentence combinations and variety are much better. Here are some good sentences from Example 3:

Deuce is a special term that means each player has three points.

Another term that is used by tennis players is *volley*.

A volley is a shot that the player hits before the ball touches the ground.

Combining Sentences with Adjective Clauses: *Who, That,* and *Which*

One way to combine two short sentences into a longer or better sentence is through the use of an adjective clause.

Reviewing Clauses

A clause is *any* group of words that includes a subject and a verb. (A sentence, for example, is a clause.) An adjective clause describes a noun. An adjective clause often begins with *who, which,* or *that.*

NOTE: Use *who* and *that* in clauses that describe people. Use *which* and *that* in clauses that describe things.

Sentences with Adjective Clauses

Study these examples. Notice how the adjective clause comes *directly after* the noun it describes.

Two sentences: Joe bought a book. The book is very easy to read.

One sentence: Joe bought a book <u>that is very easy to read</u>.
ADJECTIVE CLAUSE

Two sentences: Mrs. Habib is a teacher. She cares about her students.

One sentence: Mrs. Habib is a teacher <u>who cares about her students</u>.
ADJECTIVE CLAUSE

Two sentences: Our family cottage is on a lake. The cottage has a tennis court.

One sentence: Our family cottage, <u>which has a tennis court</u>, is on a lake.
ADJECTIVE CLAUSE

Note the comma before *which*. Use a comma when the information in the adjective clause is not necessary for the reader to identify the person, place, or thing. In other words, we use commas when the information in the adjective clause is considered extra or unnecessary.

| Activity 1 | Practice with Adjective Clauses |

Write that, who, *or* which *on the lines.*

Paragraph 55

An Old Family Photo

This is an old photo of my family. In fact, this is a photo (**1.**) _____ was taken

about sixty years ago. I remember the old sofa, (**2.**) _____ was in my parents' liv-

ing room. The two women (**3.**) _____ are sitting on the sofa are my mother and

my grandmother. The woman (**4.**) _____ has curly hair is my grandmother. My

mother, (**5.**) _____ has long hair, is to the right of my grandmother. The little

boy (**6.**) _____ is on the sofa is Uncle Bob. The sofa in the picture is really old. In

fact, this is the sofa (**7.**) _____ my grandmother received from her mother years

before. The man (**8.**) _____ is standing behind my grandmother is my grandfather.

The two men (**9.**) _____ are to the right of my grandfather are my father and Uncle

Sam. The cat (**10.**) _____ you see under the sofa was my mother's pet. The name

(**11.**) _____ my mother gave her cat was Butterball because it was such a big, fat

cat. This picture is so important to me because all of the people (**12.**) _____ I

love the most are in it. **Certainly** this is a picture (**13.**) _____ I will **cherish** for

many more years.

certainly: without doubt   **cherish:** to treat with tenderness

WRITER'S NOTE: Use *Who* or *That* for People

Remember that adjective clauses that begin with *who* describe *people* only.
Adjective clauses that begin with *that* can be for *people* or *things*. Finally, use *which* to
describe *things*.

Incorrect:	I bought a cat who is white and brown.
Correct:	I bought a cat that is white and brown.
Incorrect:	Many people which watch basketball on TV also watch football.
Correct:	Many people who watch basketball on TV also watch football.

Activity 2   Adjective Clauses at the End of a Sentence

*In each item, combine the two sentences into one by using an adjective clause. Add the second
sentence to the end of the first one, using who, which, or that. The first one has been done for you.*

1. The hula hoop was a toy. The hula hoop was popular in the 1960s.

   The hula hoop was a toy that was popular in the 1960s.

2. New Hampshire is a small state. New Hampshire is in the northeastern part of the United States.

   _____

3. Romansch is a language. Romansch comes from Latin.

   _____

4. Bolivia is a country in South America. Bolivia does not have a coastline.

   _____

5. Nasi lemak is a Malaysian dish. Nasi lemak uses white rice and coconut milk.

   _____

6. Dante Alighieri was an Italian writer. Dante Alighieri wrote *The Divine Comedy*.

   _____

7. A meerkat is a rodent. It is a native of Africa.

   _____

   _____

   _____

8. The *Titanic* was a ship. It sank in the North Atlantic Ocean.

   _____

   _____

   _____

9. A coach is a person. A coach trains athletes to perform well in sports.

   _____

   _____

   _____

10. El Prado is a famous museum. It is in the heart of Madrid, Spain.

    _____

| Activity 3 | Sentence Combining: Adjective Clauses in the Middle of a Sentence |

In each item, combine the two sentences into one by using an adjective clause. Use the second piece of information in the middle of your new sentence. The first one has been done for you.

1. The food is called hummus. I like this food the best.

   The food that I like the best is hummus.

2. The movie was *Steel Magnolias*. We saw this movie on television last night.

3. The day was October 11. We arrived in Texas on this day.

4. The number was incorrect. Paul gave me this number.

5. The story was extremely interesting. Samir told this story.

6. The homework assignment was difficult. The grammar teacher gave us the homework assignment.

7. The man is my friend. The man is standing on the street corner.

8. The food got cold. We bought the food for dinner.

9. The police officer was very angry. The police officer gave me a speeding ticket.

10. The play is very popular in London. We are going to see this play tonight.

| Activity 4 | Identifying Adjective Clauses in a Paragraph |

Read this paragraph and underline the three sentences that have adjective clauses.

Paragraph 56

EXAMPLE PARAGRAPH

A Possible Problem with the Schools

The school **district** in our city has a problem. The teachers who work in the city's schools say they might go on **strike**. The problem is money. The teachers want to go on strike because they get **salaries** that are very low. The teachers say the salaries are not fair, and they want the school **officials** to **raise** teachers' salaries. There will be an emergency meeting of the school board this evening, and the public is invited. The teachers hope the people who attend the meeting will agree with them about the low salaries. Will the teachers go on strike? We are going to learn the answer to this question at tonight's meeting.

district: an official area or community

strike: to protest by not working

salary: money that a person earns

officials: directors, leaders

raise: to make higher

| Activity 5 | Examining Adjective Clauses |

Look at the three sentences that you underlined in Activity 4. Copy each of them below. Then write the two short sentences that were combined to make the longer sentence.

Sentence 1: _____

    a. _____

    b. _____

Sentence 2: _____

    a. _____

    b. _____

Sentence 3: _____

    a. _____

    b. _____

Activity 6   **Sentence Combining: Adjective Clauses**

Each paragraph is missing a sentence. Create the missing sentence from the sentences below the paragraph. Use all the ideas but not necessarily all the words. Your new sentence should have an adjective clause and be a good supporting sentence. Write your new sentence on the lines in the paragraph.

Paragraph 57

How the Weather Affects Me

Some people don't believe that the weather can **affect** the way you feel. The weather certainly affects me. On rainy days, I feel like watching a movie or staying in bed. Rainy weather makes me **lazy**. It makes me want to stay inside and take it easy. When the weather is bright and sunny, I feel energetic. This kind of weather makes me want to go outside. I want to play tennis. I want to go to the beach. When the temperature is cool and the sun is shining, I feel like working. I feel **productive**. _____

_____

As you can see, different kinds of weather have different effects on me.

affect: to change in some way   **lazy**: not active   **productive**: able to get things done

Missing sentence ideas: <u>This is the weather</u>.   +   <u>I like this weather the most</u>.

Paragraph 58

Some English Spelling Problems

Some English words are difficult to spell. One word that many people misspell is *receive.*

Receive is a problem because some people write the *i* before the *e: recieve.* The correct spelling

is *receive* with the *e* before the *i.* _____

_____

Some people **confuse** *its* with *it's.* In addition, some people write the word *its* with an apostrophe:

its'. However, this last example is not an English word. Another example of bad spelling is

cemetery. Some people change the last *e* to *a* because of the pronunciation: *cemetary.* These are

just a few of the words that cause spelling problems for native and nonnative English speakers.

confuse: to mix without order   **cemetery:** a place where people are buried after they die

Missing sentence ideas: <u>Another word is the word *its.*</u> + <u>This word causes spelling</u>
<u>problems.</u>

Editing

| Activity 7 | **Editing: Error Correction and Sequencing** |

The sentences below have some errors in capitalization and punctuation. First, find and correct the errors in each sentence. After you have corrected the errors, put the sentences in the correct order (1 through 6). The first one has been done for you.

a. ___1___   S̶udan is a country that is in the northeastern part of ȧfrica.

b. _____   it is a large country with many different people

c. _____   in conclusion, different areas of this country have very different histories

d. _____   the people who live in the southern part of the country were independent for many years

e. _____   however, the people who live in the northern part of the country were under foreign
             control for long periods of time

f. _____   some of the countries that ruled this northern area were egypt rome turkey and britain

Activity 8	Copying Sentences

Copy the sentences from Activity 7 in correct paragraph form. Be sure to add a title.

_____

_____

_____

_____

_____

_____

_____

_____

_____

_____

UNDERSTANDING PLACE PHRASES

You learned that to make a sentence more interesting, it is important to add details such as adjectives and connectors. In Unit 6, you learned that *time words* can add variety to your sentences. Another way to give more information in a sentence is to add place phrases.

GRAMMAR AND SENTENCE STRUCTURE:
Place Phrases

Place phrases function as adverbs—they modify a verb. They tell *where*. Here are some examples.

at the picnic	on the table	under the chair	next to the door
in my house	over my head	behind the door	near the stove

Notice that the phrases begin with small words such as *at*, *in*, and *on*. These words are called prepositions. (See Appendix 10 for preposition rules.) The whole phrase tells where the action of the verb occurs.

It is common to put place phrases at the end of a sentence.

Incorrect: We ate <u>at the picnic</u> lots of hot dogs and hamburgers.

Correct: We ate lots of hot dogs and hamburgers <u>at the picnic</u>.

Incorrect: Loretta <u>in my house</u> lives.

Correct: Loretta lives <u>in my house</u>.

Place Phrases and Time Words

In sentences where you have a place phrase and a time word or phrase, remember this rule.

At the end of a sentence, place phrases usually come *before* time words or phrases.

Incorrect: Meet me <u>tomorrow afternoon</u> <u>in the backyard</u>.
                                    TIME WORDS   PLACE PHRASE

Correct: Meet me <u>in the backyard</u> <u>tomorrow afternoon</u>.
                              PLACE PHRASE   TIME WORDS

Incorrect: She saw him <u>at 8 P.M.</u> <u>at the bank</u>.
                                        ADV. TIME   ADV. PLACE

Correct: She saw him <u>at the bank</u> <u>at 8 P.M.</u>
                                    ADV. PLACE   ADV. TIME

Correct: <u>At 8 P.M.</u>, she saw him <u>at the bank</u>.
                      ADV. TIME   ADV. PLACE

Activity 9   Practicing with Place Phrases and Time Words

Read the sentence parts below. Put the parts in the correct order. Then write the complete sentences in the lines provided. You may have to add articles or verbs to the phrases. The first one has been done for you.

1. Lucinda / in ten minutes / going to / drive to / video store

   Lucinda is going to drive to the video store in ten minutes.

2. last week / the Johnson sisters / party / excellent / have

   _____

3. next Monday / new car / we / buy

_____

4. at gym / exercise / Janie / every morning

_____

5. did you take / yesterday morning / in Mrs. Smith's class/ grammar test

_____ ?

6. leave / I / last night / my books / in car

_____

7. two days ago / met Luis / they / at restaurant

_____

8. Sara / the pie / right now / put / in oven

_____

9. at airport / in ten minutes / our friends / arrive

_____

10. squirrels / every day / nuts / bury / under our oak tree

_____

Activity 10	**Practicing Adverbs of Place and Time Words**

Read the paragraph. It is missing three sentences. Below the paragraph are the missing sentences. Put the words in each sentence in the correct order. Then write the complete sentences in the spaces provided. You will have to add articles and the correct verb tense.

Paragraph 58

A Long Flight

(**1.**) _____

_____

However, Daniel lives in La Paz, Bolivia, so he must take an airplane to Turkey before the meeting. Daniel is going to go to the airport today. (**2.**) _____

_____

Because Daniel is going to take an international flight, he has to be at the airport at 3:00 P.M. If he doesn't leave his house by noon, he is going to be late. It is almost 11:30 now. (**3.**) _____

_____

_____

Then he will leave on his long trip.

1. attend / in Istanbul, Turkey / Daniel / important company meeting / in two days
2. his flight / at 5:00 P.M. / leave / from Gate 32
3. his suitcase / Daniel / put / in ten minutes / in the car

| **Activity 11** | **Sentence or Fragment Review** |

Read each group of words. If it is a fragment, write F on the line. If it is a complete sentence, write S on the line. The first two have been done for you.

1. ___F___ Every year go to the beach in Hawaii.

2. ___S___ Johnny has an appointment with a chiropractor at 4:30 P.M.

3. _____ Japan and South Korea are going to host the 2002 World Cup Soccer Tournament.

4. _____ Ten years to become a medical doctor in the United States.

5. _____ Next Tuesday am going to see the new Steven Spielberg film.

6. _____ Did you get a nice gift for your birthday last week?

7. _____ Wendy is eating lunch and talking to her friends in the cafeteria right now.

8. _____ Because the concert didn't end at 10 P.M.

9. _____ Peru and Argentina Spanish-speaking countries in the Southern Hemisphere.

10. _____ Ralph left his wallet at his friend's house last night.

Editing

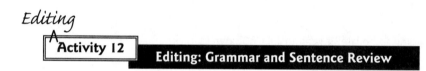

Activity 12   **Editing: Grammar and Sentence Review**

Read the following paragraph. It contains ten mistakes: adjective clauses (1), fragments (1), word order-adjectives (1), possessive adjectives (1), commas (2), articles (1), compound sentences (1), and capitalization (2). Find and correct the mistakes. The first one has been done for you.

Paragraph 59

Visiting a New Country

There are m

~~M~~any reasons to visit a new country. First, you can see beautiful interesting and distant

places. For example, you can visit a Kremlin and Red Square in moscow. Another reason to travel

is to eat new types of food. If you visit Thailand, you can drink jasmine tea, you can eat

coconut-flavored rice. Finally, you can meet new people which live in these exotic countries. you

can talk to people and learn more about his likes and dislikes. As you can see, traveling to

another country is important for reasons different.

Activity 13 | Original Writing Practice

In your opinion, which is better—cooking and eating food at home or eating out in a restaurant? Write a paragraph in which you answer this question and tell why.

Then follow these steps for writing, and use the checklist. Put a check (✓) next to each step as you complete it. You may want to review What Is a Paragraph? in Unit 2 on page 34.

Step 1 _____ In your first sentence, tell which type of food you prefer.

Step 2 _____ In the supporting sentences, give two or three reasons to describe why you prefer this type of food.

Step 3 _____ Give details for each reason you give.

Step 4 _____ In the last sentence, summarize your opinion about the type of food that you prefer.

Step 5 _____ Write at least two adjective clauses.

Step 6 _____ Try to include time words and place phrases in some of the sentences in Step 2 or Step 3.

Step 7 _____ Write at least one compound and one complex sentence in Step 2 or Step 3.

Checklist

✔ 1. ❑ Did you use simple present tense in your paragraph?

✔ 2. ❑ Make sure that you use articles correctly.

✔ 3. ❑ Check for correct punctuation.

✔ 4. ❑ Make sure every sentence has a subject and a verb—no fragments!

✔ 5. ❑ Create a title for your paragraph.

Activity 14   **Peer Editing**

Choose someone that you work well with. Exchange papers from Activity 13 with that student. Read your partner's paragraph. Use Peer Editing Sheet 7 on page 231 to help you talk about your partner's work.

Activity 15   **Journal Writing**

Here are ten ideas for journal writing. Choose one or more of them to write about. Follow your teacher's directions. (We recommend that you skip a line after each line that you write. This gives your teacher a place to write comments.)

1. Write about an animal that you like. Describe the animal, tell where the animal lives, and tell why you like this animal so much.

2. Write about your dream house or apartment. Describe what this house looks like (how many rooms, what type of architecture, etc.). Write about the location of the house (in the mountains? on the beach? in a big city?).

3. Organized sports in school help children grow up to become better adults. Do you agree or disagree with this statement? Why?

4. Do you think that young children who know something about computers have an advantage in school today? Why or why not?

5. What is the worst decision that you ever made? Give details about why it was a bad decision.

6. What is the best decision that you ever made? Why was it a good decision? Did you come to this decision by yourself? How did you feel after you made this decision?

EXTRA WRITING

7. Write about a book that you like. Describe the book, briefly tell what happens in the story, and tell why you like this book.

8. Describe a painting that you like. Who painted it? What is in the painting? Describe colors. What do you feel when you look at the painting?

9. Describe your favorite kind of shopping. Where do you shop? What do you shop for? What do you like about the experience?

10. Describe your favorite place to visit. Where is this place? When do you go there? Why do you go there?

EXTRA WRITING

Unit 8

More Practice with Sentences and Paragraphs

GOAL: To practice sentence and paragraph skills from Units 1–7

PRACTICE WITH SENTENCES AND PARAGRAPHS

This unit contains twenty-four activities for practicing writing great sentences in great paragraphs. Some activities focus on sentences while others focus on paragraphs.

When you write the paragraphs in this unit, keep these things in mind:

Important Parts of a Paragraph

TOPIC SENTENCE	1. A good paragraph has a topic sentence that states the main idea.
Only ONE TOPIC	2. All of the sentences in the paragraph are about one topic.
INDENTED line	3. The first line of a paragraph is indented.
BODY AND SUPPORTING SENTENCES	4. A good paragraph has a sufficient number of supporting sentences.
CONCLUDING SENTENCE	5. The last sentence, or concluding sentence, brings the paragraph to a logical conclusion.

| Practice 1 | Basic Punctuation and Capitalization |

Read each set of sentences. Correct the punctuation and capitalization errors. Then number the sentences in the correct order. Rewrite the sentences in paragraph form on the lines below. Finally, add a title.

A.

a. _____ in fact, the andes affect almost every aspect of peruvian life

b. _____ it is located in the south-central part of the continent

c. _____ peru is a country in south America

d. _____ the andes mountains run through the middle of the country

e. _____ the mountains affect weather agriculture and transportation

_____

_____

_____

_____

_____

_____

_____

_____

_____

B.

    a. _____ they are classified as birds but they cannot fly

    b. _____ instead, they are excellent swimmers because they have wings shaped like flippers

    c. _____ they live only in the cold regions in the southern hemisphere

    d. _____ penguins are very interesting animals

    e. _____ many people think that these birds live at the north pole but they do not

_____

_____

_____

_____

_____

_____

_____

_____

_____

Practice 2	Word Forms

This activity will help you practice correct noun and adjective forms, verb tense, and article usage. Read the paragraph. Underline the word that correctly completes each sentence.

Paragraph 60

The Tomato: Fruit or Vegetable?

In supermarkets, people can find tomatoes in the vegetable section, but this common food

is actually a (**1.** fruit / fruits). Many people (**2.** believe / believes) it is a (**3.** vegetable because /

vegetable. Because) we eat it with (**4.** others / other) salty foods. For example, we eat (**5.** tomato

/ tomatoes) in a salad or on sandwiches. We don't eat (**6.** tomato / tomatoes) for dessert or with

anything sweet. However, the tomato is (**7.** really a / a really) fruit. Now isn't that strange?

| **Practice 3** | **Editing in Four Steps** |

Read this paragraph. Then rewrite it according to the four editing steps below.

Paragraph 61

EXAMPLE PARAGRAPH

Our Family's Koi Pond

Today my father is going to build a koi pond in our backyard. First, he is going to dig a big hole in the center of the yard. Then he is going to lay a sheet of black plastic in the hole. Next, he is going to put rocks around the edge of the hole. After that, he is going to fill the new pond with water. Finally, he is going to add plants and fish. It is going to be a lot of hard work, but he is going to enjoy it.

Make the following changes to the paragraph above. Write your new paragraph on the lines below.

Step 1. In the first sentence, change *my father* to *my father and I.*

Step 2. Change all the pronouns to fit the new subject.

Step 3. In the first sentence, change the word *Today* to *Last Saturday.*

Step 4. Change all the future tense verbs to past tense verbs.

Our Family's Koi Pond

_____

_____

_____

_____

_____

_____

_____

_____

Practice 4	Editing in Five Steps

Read this paragraph. Then rewrite it according to the five editing steps below.

Paragraph 62

EXAMPLE PARAGRAPH

Our First Garden

Two years ago, my brother and I planted our first garden. First, we chose the location of the garden. We put it in a place that gets a lot of sunlight. Then we dug up the ground. After that, we added fertilizer. Next, we took seeds and planted them in rows in the garden. Finally, we watered the new garden. It was hard work, but we are proud of our garden.

Make the following changes to the paragraph above. Write your new paragraph on the lines below.

Step 1. In the first sentence, change *my brother and I* to *Antonio*.

Step 2. Change all the pronouns and possessive words to fit the new subject.

Step 3. In the first sentence, change the phrase *Two years ago* to *Tomorrow*.

Step 4. Change all the past tense verbs to future tense verbs (*be going to*).

Step 5. Check the other verbs to make sure that they are correct.

Antonio's First Garden

_____

_____

_____

_____

_____

_____

_____

_____

Practice 5 **Verb Forms**

This activity will help you practice choosing the correct verb tense. Read the paragraph. Underline the correct verbs. Then answer the questions that follow the paragraph.

Paragraph 63

An Important Invention

I (**1.** believe / believed) that the light bulb is one of the most important inventions in the world. In the past, people (**2.** used / are using) candles to see at night. This light was very weak and difficult to see with. However, the light bulb now (**3.** allowed / allows) us to see things easily in the dark. This invention also (**4.** help / helps) us to do more work in one day. Before the light bulb, most work (**5.** ends / ended) at sundown. Now people can continue to work outdoors or in their offices for much longer at night. In addition, people can do more fun things when it is dark. For example, sports fans (**6.** watch / watched) baseball games at night on lighted fields. Music lovers (**7.** listen / are listening) to a concert in a lighted stadium. Without the light bulb, people would not have as many choices for work or play.

1. What is the topic sentence of the paragraph?

   _____

   _____

2. How many sentences does the paragraph have? _____

3. What reasons does the writer give to support the main idea?

   _____

   _____

4. What two verb tenses does the writer use? Why?

   _____

   _____

| Practice 6 | **Original Writing Practice with Verb Tenses** |

In Practice 5, you read about one writer's opinion about an important invention in history. What do you think is an important invention in history? Write a short paragraph about it. Include a topic sentence and three examples to support your opinion. Create a title for your paragraph.

_____

_____

_____

_____

_____

_____

_____

| Practice 7 | **Verb Tense** |

This activity will help you practice choosing the correct verb tense. Read the paragraph. Underline the correct verbs.

Paragraph 64

A Busy Day

Tomorrow (**1.** is / is going to be) a busy day for me. Usually, I (**2.** get / am getting) up at seven o'clock in the morning. However, tomorrow I (**3.** get / am going to get) up at five o'clock because I am going to go to the gym. After I finish at the gym, I (**4.** go / am going to go) to work. I usually (**5.** start / am starting) work at nine o'clock. Tomorrow I (**6.** start / am going to start) work at eight o'clock. After work, I frequently (**7.** have / am having) dinner with my friends. However, tomorrow I (**8.** go / am going to go) directly to my mother's house because it is her birthday. We (**9.** have / are going to have) a big party for her. I know I will have a lot of fun tomorrow.

1. What is the topic sentence of the paragraph?

   _____

   _____

2. How many sentences does the paragraph have? _____

3. What reasons does the writer give to support the main idea?

   _____

   _____

4. What two tenses does the writer use? Why?

   _____

   _____

Practice 8	**Original Writing Practice with Verb Tense**

In Practice 7, you read about one person's busy day. Write a paragraph. Describe a busy day in your life. It can be about a day in the past, present, or future. Include a topic sentence and three examples to support your opinion. Create a title for your work.

_____

_____

_____

_____

_____

_____

_____

Practice 9	Articles

This activity will help you review the correct use of articles. Read the paragraph. Underline the article that correctly completes each sentence. (Note: ø means "no article.")

Paragraph 65

Shark!

I'll never forget my first encounter with (**1.** a / an / ø) shark. I was sixteen, and I was visiting Australia with my family. My father and I went scuba diving on (**2.** a / the / ø) Great Barrier Reef. We went out to (**3.** a / the / ø) reef with many other tourists on (**4.** a / an / the) special boat. When we got to (**5.** a / the / ø) reef, the scuba diving instructor helped us put on our equipment. Then we dove into (**6.** a / the / ø) clear blue water. Everything was so beautiful! There were colorful fish and lots of different kinds of coral. I swam everywhere. Suddenly, I saw (**7.** a / an / the) huge gray shark swim towards me. I looked around for my father, but I was far away from him and (**8.** a / an / the) group of tourists. What could I do? (**9.** A / An / The) shark got closer and closer. I was so scared that I couldn't move. Just when I thought that it might bite me, (**10.** a / an / the) shark turned and swam (**11.** a / the / ø) other way. Unbelievable! I quickly found my father. Now I never swim off by myself when I go scuba diving.

Editing

Practice 10	Editing for Articles

Follow these instructions:

1. Reread your writing in Practice 6 and Practice 8.
2. Choose four sentences from your paragraphs that contain articles. Write them below.
3. Ask a partner to check your sentences. Did you use articles correctly?

_____

_____

_____

_____

_____

_____

_____

WRITER'S NOTE: Add Interest to Your Writing

Remember to use a variety of sentence types (simple, compound, complex) in your writing. Different kinds of sentences will make your writing more interesting. You can also use adverbs and adjectives to add variety and interest to your writing.

| Practice 11 | **Connecting Sentences in a Paragraph** |

This activity will help you practice combining sentences with a connector. Combine each underlined pair of sentences. You may use and, but, *or* so *to connect them. Remember to add a comma before the connecting word. You may have to delete some words. Rewrite the paragraph on the lines below.*

Paragraph 66

My First Car

My first car was the best car in the world. It was a Ford Mustang. (**1.**) <u>My Mustang was bright blue</u>. <u>It was very powerful</u>. All my friends were jealous when they saw it. (**2.**) <u>They wanted to drive it</u>. <u>I told them they could not</u>. I said that they could be passengers or pedestrians. (**3.**) <u>My friends didn't want to walk</u>. <u>They always chose to be passengers</u>. However, the best thing about my car was the way it made me feel. (**4.**) <u>Every weekend I drove to the movie theater in that car</u>. <u>Every weekend my friends rode with me</u>. We felt like movie stars because everyone stared at us in the beautiful blue car. I will never forget the fun that I had in that cool car.

_____

_____

_____

_____

_____

_____

_____

_____

Editing

Practice 12   **Editing for Connectors (*and, but, so*)**

Follow these instructions:

1. Reread your writing in Practice 6 and Practice 8. Did you use any connectors in your sentences?

2. If so, rewrite those sentences below.

3. If not, combine two of your sentences with a connector.

4. Ask a partner to check your sentences. Did you use connectors correctly?

_____

_____

_____

_____

_____

_____

| Practice 13 | **Adjective Clauses with *Who / That / Which*** |

Read the paragraph. Underline the word that correctly completes each sentence.

Paragraph 65

How the Months of the Year Got Their Names

The names of all twelve months come from Roman culture and myths. First, there are several months (**1.** that / whom) are named after Roman gods and goddesses. The Roman god (**2.** who / which) gave us the month of January is Janus, god of beginnings. The month (**3.** that / who) got its name from the Roman god of war is March. May and June honor the Roman goddesses Maia and Juno. Some months got their names from festivals. Both February and April come from special celebrations (**4.** that / whom) appeared on the old Roman calendar. Two months (**5.** whom / that) come in the summer got their names from Roman emperors. July is the month (**6.** that / who) honors Julius Caesar, and August is named for Emperor Augustus. Finally, September, October, November, and December are named after the seventh, eighth, ninth, and tenth months of the Roman calendar. Month names (**7.** that / who) are so commonly used today have a very rich history.

Editing

Practice 14   **Editing for Adjective Clauses**

Follow these instructions:

1. Reread your writing in Practice 6 and Practice 8. Did you use adjective clauses in your writing?

2. If so, rewrite those sentences below.

3. If not, combine two of your sentences using an adjective clause.

4. Ask a partner to check your sentences. Did you use adjective clauses correctly?

_____

_____

_____

_____

Practice 15   **Topic Sentences and Supporting Sentences**

*This activity will help you recognize the difference between a topic sentence and supporting sentences. Each pair of sentences is about one topic. Decide which sentence is the topic sentence (T) and which is a supporting sentence (S). (*Hint: *The topic sentence gives more general information.)*

1. Topic: Kennedy Space Center

    _____ You can visit the Shuttle Plaza and walk through a life-size model of a space shuttle.

    _____ Kennedy Space Center is a great place to visit.

2. Topic: The Definition of Patience

    _____ A teacher often shows patience to young students at the end of the school day.

    _____ Patience is the ability to continue doing something even if you do not see any results immediately.

3. Topic: The Capilano Bridge

    _____ The Capilano Bridge is famous worldwide.

    _____ The Capilano Bridge is 450 feet (137 m) long and rises 230 feet (70 m) above the Capilano River.

4. Topic: Making New Friends

_____ Some kids tried to be nice to me, but I didn't want to talk to them.

_____ I learned the hard way how to make friends in a new school.

5. Topic: Cellular Phones and Driving

_____ When drivers talk on cell phones, they get distracted and don't pay enough attention to driving.

_____ One of the recent developments of modern technology, cellular phones, can be a threat to safe driving.

Practice 16 **Sentence Order in Paragraphs**

Read all the sentences below. Then put them in a logical paragraph order. When you finish, write the sentences in correct paragraph format on the lines below. Be sure to add an appropriate title.

a. _____ Instead, breakfast often consists of eggs with toast and coffee.

b. _____ People in Malaysia eat rice for breakfast, too, but their rice is cooked in coconut milk.

c. _____ Breakfast foods vary from country to country.

d. _____ However, people in most countries in Central and South America do not eat rice for breakfast.

e. _____ People eat this sweet, flavored rice with a red paste that is made of ground chili peppers and other ingredients.

f. _____ In Japan, for example, it is common to eat rice, soup, and fish for breakfast.

g. _____ From these varied breakfast items, it is clear that breakfast foods are different around the world.

_____

_____

_____

_____

_____

_____

_____

_____

_____

_____

_____

_____

_____

Practice 17	Pre-reading Questions

Discuss the answers to these questions in a small group. Then read the paragraph.

1. Do you like to cook? If so, what is your favorite meal to prepare?

2. How much time do you spend in the kitchen?

3. Have you ever eaten linguine?

Paragraph 68

Something Easy to Cook

EXAMPLE PARAGRAPH

One of the quickest and easiest meals to prepare is linguine with tomato sauce. First, fill a large pot about three-quarters of the way with water. Bring the water to a boil and add about eight ounces of your favorite linguine. It will take about ten minutes for the pasta to cook thoroughly. While the pasta is cooking, heat a large skillet with about two tablespoons of olive oil. Slice three or four cloves of garlic and add them to the skillet. Stir frequently until the garlic cloves become a golden brown color. Add a large can of tomato sauce to the garlic and oil. Then add a pinch of salt and pepper. When the linguine is done, strain it in a colander, then put the linguine in the skillet. Add some grated parmesan cheese and some chopped basil. Your delicious linguine dinner is ready. *Buon appetito!*

Practice 18	Analyzing the Paragraph

Read each question about Paragraph 68 in Practice 17. Circle the best answer.

1. What is the main topic of the paragraph?

   a. The health benefits of linguine

   b. Why linguine is inexpensive

   c. Cooking a quick linguine meal

2. What is the topic sentence of this paragraph?

    a. One of the quickest and easiest meals to prepare is linguine with tomato sauce.

    b. First, fill a large pot about three-quarters of the way with water.

    c. Add some grated parmesan cheese and some chopped basil.

3. In your opinion, what does the paragraph explain?

    a. It explains why cooking linguine is better than eating fast food.

    b. It tells you that linguine is the easiest and most delicious food to make in the kitchen.

    c. It lists the steps necessary to make a quick linguine dinner.

4. How many (food) ingredients does the author mention in the paragraph?

    a. Three

    b. Seven

    c. Ten

5. Read the paragraph again. What verb tense is most often used?

    a. Simple past

    b. Simple present

    c. Future

WRITER'S NOTE: Words That Express an Opinion

When you write about your beliefs on a subject, you are giving your *opinion*. Here are some words that you can use when you write about your opinion:

believe	I *believe* that no one should smoke in public.
feel	I *feel* that smoking is a personal decision.
think	I *think* that smoking is bad for your health.
agree	I *agree* with the new laws that prohibit smoking.
disagree	I *disagree* with the new laws that prohibit smoking.
have mixed feelings	I *have mixed feelings* about smoking in public places. (This means the writer has more than one opinion on the topic and the opinions conflict with each other.)

RESPONDING TO ISSUES IN THE NEWS

In the following section, you will read paragraphs that discuss topics in the news. You will also read people's opinions on these issues. Then you will write about your opinions.

Practice 19   **Responding to a Reading Passage**

Read the following paragraph. Then read the opinions that follow and answer the questions.

Paragraph 69

EXAMPLE PARAGRAPH

Smoking in Public Places

In the late 1990s, several U.S. cities voted **to ban** smoking in restaurants and bars. The main reason for doing this was public health. The action was **controversial** because smokers felt **discriminated against**. Some **activists** believe that **barring** smokers from these public **establishments** is not the only solution to the problem. In fact, they propose establishing separate areas for smokers and nonsmokers, installing advanced ventilation systems, and using other measures. However, the **ruling** to ban smoking in public places is now a law.

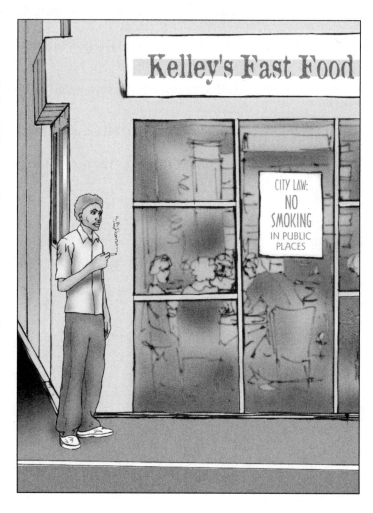

to ban: to prohibit; to make illegal

controversial: causing conflict or debate

discriminated against: judged or acted upon unfavorably

activist: someone who works to support a political cause

barring: prohibiting; banning

establishment: business

ruling: decision

Opinion 1

Melinda:

Because second-hand smoke causes cancer, I believe that banning smoking in restaurants and bars is correct. If smoking is not allowed in buildings such as post offices and banks, why should it be any different for restaurants and bars? One day smoking is going to be against the law, so this is not going to be an issue anymore. Until then, the smokers must smoke outside.

1. What is the topic sentence of Melinda's paragraph?

_____

_____

2. In your own words, write one sentence about how Melinda feels about this issue.

_____

_____

3. What argument does Melinda use to support her opinion?

_____

_____

Opinion 2

Scott:

I'm not a smoker, but I disagree with the new laws that prohibit smoking. I think it's unfair to single out smokers and make them feel unaccepted. People in bars and restaurants can drink too much and possibly get into fatal car accidents, and that is much worse than smoking. I feel bad for smokers because they cannot smoke when they want to. I think that fewer smokers are going to go out to restaurants and bars because of this law.

1. What is the topic sentence of Scott's paragraph?

_____

_____

2. In your own words, write one sentence about how Scott feels about this issue.

_____

_____

3. What argument does Scott use to support his opinion?

_____

_____

Opinion 3

Amanda:

I really have mixed feelings about this new law. On the one hand, I'm glad that when I go into a bar my eyes don't burn from the cigarette smoke. Sometimes bars are so smoky that you cannot see one foot in front of you. On the other hand, I believe that there can be a compromise. I go to some restaurants with smoking and nonsmoking areas, and I have no problems there. Maybe the two groups can reach a compromise that will satisfy everyone.

1. What is the topic sentence of Amanda's paragraph?

   _____

   _____

2. In your own words, write one sentence about how Amanda feels about this issue.

   _____

   _____

3. How is Amanda's opinion different from Melinda's and Scott's?

   _____

   _____

WRITER'S NOTE: *Should* and the Tone of Verbs

You can use the word *should* to soften your verbs when you give your opinion. For example:

Too strong:	People <u>must</u> not talk on their cellular phones in their cars.
Too strong:	People <u>need</u> to stop talking on their cellular phones in their cars.
Softer:	People <u>should</u> not talk on their cellular phone in their cars.

Practice 20   Original Writing

Now it's your turn to state your opinion about this issue. Write a paragraph that tells if you support or oppose the idea of banning smoking in restaurants and bars. Indent your paragraph.

Careful! Be sure that the first sentence (the topic sentence) states your opinion. Include good supporting sentences. Give your paragraph a title.

   _____

   _____

   _____

_____

_____

_____

_____

_____

_____

_____

_____

_____

WRITER'S NOTE: Editing

Remember that it is very important to edit your writing. When you edit your writing, you find and correct your mistakes. You should also ask other people to edit your work. They may find mistakes that you missed.

Practice 21   **Peer Editing**

Exchange papers from Practice 20 with another student. Read your partner's paragraph. Use Peer Editing Sheet 8 on page 233 to help you talk about your partner's work.

Practice 22   **Responding to a Reading Passage**

Read the following paragraph. Then read the opinions that follow and answer the questions.

Paragraph 70

EXAMPLE PARAGRAPH

A Medical Dilemma

Recently, there was a **controversy** in Great Britain involving **conjoined twins**. A woman from Malta gave birth to baby girls. Unfortunately, these girls were attached to each other. The parents, who were strict Catholics, did not want doctors to separate the babies. They said it was murder. The doctors explained that with the operation, one baby would live. Without the operation, both babies would die. The British court made the final decision. The doctors performed the operation, and one of the babies died.

controversy: debate or conflict   conjoined twins: twins that are physically attached

Opinion 1

Joseph:

A court must not have more power over someone's children than the family. It is unbelievable that the court forced its decision on this unlucky family. The birth of these girls was a natural event, and it was destiny that they were born conjoined twins. The parents didn't want the operation because of their religion. That is a strong enough reason to let the parents make the final decision.

1. What is the topic sentence of Joseph's paragraph?

   _____

   _____

2. In your own words, write one sentence about how Joseph feels about this case.

   _____

   _____

3. What argument does Joseph use to support his idea?

   _____

   _____

Opinion 2

Rebecca:

When a human life is involved, the court must have some power in making the decision. Of course the case of these conjoined twin girls is a tragedy, but modern science could help them! The parents used their religion to make the decision. The court only wanted to save a human life. Maybe the parents didn't realize that both little girls would die without the operation. To save one baby, I agree with the court.

1. What is the topic sentence of Rebecca's paragraph?

   _____

   _____

2. In your own words, write one sentence about how Rebecca feels about this case.

_____

_____

3. What argument does Rebecca use to support her idea?

_____

_____

WRITER'S NOTE: Vary Your Vocabulary

Vocabulary is a key part of good writing. Your level of vocabulary is an indication of your English proficiency. The reader's opinion of your writing will be higher if you use better vocabulary. Variety is important. In your paragraphs, try to use synonyms, phrases, and sometimes whole sentences to say the same information in a different way. Avoid using the same words all the time.

Practice 23   **Original Writing**

Now it's your turn to state your opinion about this case. Tell if you agree or not with what the court decided about the twins.

Careful! Be sure that the first sentence you write (topic sentence) states the opinion you agree with. Include good supporting sentences. Give your paragraph a title.

_____

_____

_____

_____

_____

_____

_____

_____

_____

_____

Practice 24   **Peer Editing**

Exchange papers from Practice 23 with another student. Read your partner's paragraph. Use Peer Editing Sheet 9 on page 235 to help you talk about your partner's work.

Appendices

Appendix I

Capitalization Rules

1. The first word in a sentence or question is capitalized.

   <u>E</u>very week I go to the movies.

   <u>D</u>o you like to play tennis?

2. The pronoun *I* is always capitalized.

   Larry and <u>I</u> are brothers.

3. People's formal and professional titles use capital letters.

   <u>M</u>r. and <u>M</u>rs. Jenkins are on vacation.

   Lisa saw <u>D</u>r. Johansen at the bank yesterday.

4. Proper names (specific people and places) use capital letters.

   The <u>C</u>oliseum in <u>R</u>ome is a beautiful old monument.

   <u>I</u>rene met her brother <u>D</u>on and his dog <u>S</u>kippy at the park.

5. Names of streets use capital letters.

   Ruth lives on <u>W</u>ilson <u>A</u>venue.

6. Geographical locations (cities, states, countries, continents, lakes, and rivers) use capital letters.

   I am going to travel to <u>L</u>ondon, <u>E</u>ngland, next week.

   The <u>A</u>rno <u>R</u>iver passes through <u>T</u>uscany, <u>I</u>taly.

7. The names of languages and nationalities use capital letters.

   My grandmother speaks <u>P</u>olish.

   Jessica is going to learn <u>J</u>apanese.

   Melisa is <u>V</u>enezuelan, but her husband is <u>C</u>uban.

8. Most words in titles of paragraphs, essays, and books are capitalized. The first letter of a title is always capitalized, and the other important words in a title are capitalized. Do not capitalize prepositions (*to*, *in*), conjunctions (*and*, *but*), or articles (*a*, *an*, *the*) unless they are the first word of the title.

   The Life of Billy Barnes

   Crime and Punishment

   The Catcher in the Rye

9. Specific course names are capitalized.

   Are you taking History 101 at 10:00 A.M.?

   Are you taking history this semester? (no capital letter)

Appendix 2

Spelling Rules for Regular Past Tense Verbs

1. Add *-ed* to the base form of most verbs.

start	started
finish	finished
wash	washed

2. Add only *-d* when the base form ends in an *e*.

live	lived
care	cared
die	died

3. If the verb ends in a consonant + *y*, change the *y* to *i* and add *-ed*.

dry	dried
carry	carried
spy	spied

4. If the verb ends in a vowel + *y*, do not change the *y*. Just add *-ed*.

pray	prayed
stay	stayed
destroy	destroyed

5. If the verb has one syllable and ends in a consonant + vowel + consonant (CVC), double the final consonant and add *-ed*.

stop	stopped
cvc	
rob	robbed
cvc	

6. Do not double final *w* or *x*.

    sew   sewed

    mix   mixed

7. If the verb has two syllables, and the final syllable is stressed, double the final consonant.

    ad mit´   admitted

    oc cur´   occurred

    per mit´   permitted

8. If the verb has two syllables, and the final syllable is *not* stressed, do *not* double the final consonant.

    hap´pen   happened

    lis´ten   listened

    o´pen   opened

Appendix 3

Irregular Past Tense Verbs

These are some of the more common irregular verbs in English.

Base Form	Simple Past	Base Form	Simple Past
be (am/is/are)	was / were	flee	fled
bite	bit	forget	forgot
bleed	bled	get	got
blow	blew	give	gave
break	broke	grow	grew
become	became	have	had
begin	began	hear	heard
bring	brought	hide	hid
build	built	hit	hit
buy	bought	hold	held
catch	caught	hurt	hurt
choose	chose	keep	kept
come	came	know	knew
cost	cost	leave	left
cut	cut	let	let
do	did	lose	lost
drink	drank	make	made
drive	drove	pay	paid
eat	ate	put	put
fall	fell	read	read
feel	felt	run	ran
fight	fought	say	said
find	found	see	saw

Base Form	Simple Past	Base Form	Simple Past
sell	sold	swim	swam
send	sent	take	took
set	set	teach	taught
sing	sang	tell	told
sit	sat	think	thought
sleep	slept	throw	threw
speak	spoke	understand	understood
spend	spent	wear	wore
stand	stood	win	won
steal	stole	write	wrote

Appendix 4

Spelling of the *-ing* (present participle) Form of Verbs

1. Add *-ing* to most verbs.

catch	catching
wear	wearing
go	going

2. If the verb ends with a consonant + *e*, drop the *e* and then add *-ing*.

write	writing
drive	driving
take	taking

3. If the verb has one syllable and ends with a consonant + a vowel + a consonant (CVC), double the final consonant.

   run   running
   CVC

   sit   sitting
   CVC

   stop   stopping
   CVC

4. Do not double *w*, *x*, or *y*.

sew	sewing
mix	mixing
say	saying

5. If the verb has two syllables and the *last* syllable is stressed, double the final consonant.

be gin´	beginning
ad mit´	admitting
re fer´	referring

6. If the verb has two syllables and the first syllable is stressed, do *not* double the final consonant.

o´pen	opening
lis´ten	listening
frigh´ten	frightening

Appendix 5

Common Stative, or Non-Action, Verbs

Below is a list of common stative, or non-action, verbs. In general, these verbs do not use the progressive tense because they do not show an action.

Incorrect: She is drinking that coffee because she is disliking green tea.

Correct: She is drinking that coffee because she <u>dislikes</u> green tea.

agree	hear	own	taste
be	know	prefer	think
believe	like	remember	understand
cost	love	see	want
dislike	mean	seem	
hate	need	smell	

Appendix 6

Definite Article *The*

Use the article *the* when you are writing about a specific noun.

1. Use *the* for the second (and subsequent) time you write about something.
   I bought a new coat yesterday. The coat is blue and gray.

2. Use *the* when the writer and the reader both know about or are familiar with the subject.
   Are you going to the bank this afternoon?
   (Both the writer and the reader know which bank they are talking about.)

3. Use *the* when the noun you are referring to is unique (there is only one).
   The sun and the Earth are both in the Milky Way galaxy.
   The Eiffel Tower is a beautiful monument.

4. Use *the* for specific nouns that are followed by a phrase.
   The history of France is long and interesting.
   The dictionary on the teacher's desk is mine.

5. Use *the* with specific time periods.
   You must be very quiet for the next hour.

6. Use *the* when the other words in your sentence make the noun specific.
   The cat in the picture is very pretty. (*in the picture* tells which cat)

7. Do not use *the* before names or when you talk about something in general.
   Andrei Bulgakov is a famous Russian writer.
   Jason is going to make a doghouse with wood.

8. Some geographic locations require *the*, but others do not. Cities, states, countries, continents, and lakes do not use *the*.

Sylvie is from <u>Venezuela</u>. She lives near <u>Lake Maracaibo</u>.
　　　　　　　COUNTRY NAME　　　　　　　　　　LAKE NAME

However, if there is an *s* (plural) or the words *united, union, kingdom,* or *republic* in the name of the country, use *the*.

We are going to <u>the Bahamas</u> for our vacation. (The country name ends with *-s*.)

Who is the president of <u>the United States</u>? (*United* is in the country name.)

Most buildings, bodies of water (except lakes), mountain chains, and deserts use *the*.

<u>The White House</u> is in Washington, D.C.
　　　BUILDING NAME

<u>The Amazon</u> is a very long river in South America.
　　RIVER NAME

<u>Lake Baikal</u> is a large fresh water lake in Russia.
LAKE NAME—NO *THE*

Appendix 7

Common Noncount Nouns

Count nouns can be counted: *three* dogs, *two* computers, *one* house, *ten* cakes. A noncount noun cannot be counted. Study these commonly used noncount nouns.

Food:	butter sugar salt pepper soup rice fish meat flour bread
Liquid:	milk coffee water juice cream
Subjects:	English math science music biology
Abstract:	love honesty poverty crime advice luck pain hate beauty humor
Others:	homework information money furniture traffic

Appendix 8

Possessive Adjectives

In general, subject pronouns come before the verb. Possessive adjectives come before a noun.

Subject Form	Possessive Adjective Form
I	my
you (singular)	your
he	his
she	her
it	its
we	our
you (plural)	your
they	their

Examples:

I went to Rome last summer with <u>my</u> family.

<u>They</u> like to eat <u>her</u> cooking.

The bird hurt <u>its</u> wing.

Bill called <u>his</u> friends.

Appendix 9

Quantifiers

Quantifiers give more information about the quantity, or number, of a noun. Quantifiers usually go in front of a noun. Here are some common examples.

one	many
two	much
three	a lot of
(all numbers)	another
some	the other
any	other
a few	several
few	a pair of
a little	a couple of
little	

Examples:

There is only a <u>little</u> time left before the end of class.

<u>Several</u> students went to the school office.

They got into <u>a lot of</u> trouble.

Appendix 10

The Prepositions *In*, *At*, and *On*

Prepositions express different ideas. They can indicate time, location, and direction. Remember that a preposition is always followed by a noun (or pronoun).

Three very common prepositions in English are *at*, *on*, and *in*. In general, we use *at* with small, specific times and places, and we use *in* with larger, more general times and places.

	Time	Place
Small:	at 1 P.M.	at McDonald's
Middle:	on Monday	on Princeton Street
Big:	in July	in Orlando
	in spring	in Florida
	in 1995	in the United States
	in this century	in North America

AT

LOCATION

Use *at* for the specific location of an object.

> Angela works <u>at</u> the First National Bank.
>
> I always do my homework <u>at</u> my desk.
>
> Jeff met Joanne <u>at</u> the corner of Polk Street and Florida Avenue.

TIME

Use *at* for specific times.

> My grammar class meets <u>at</u> 9:00 A.M. every day.
>
> I'll see you <u>at</u> noon for lunch!
>
> Carla doesn't like to walk alone <u>at</u> night.

DIRECTION

Use *at* for motion toward a goal.

My brother threw a ball <u>at</u> me.

The robber pointed his gun <u>at</u> the policewoman.

ON

LOCATION

Use *on* when there is contact between two objects. We also use *on* with streets.

The picture is <u>on</u> the wall.

He puts his books <u>on</u> the kitchen table.

Candice lives <u>on</u> Bayshore Boulevard.

TIME

Use *on* with specific days or dates.

Our soccer game is <u>on</u> Saturday.

Your dentist appointment is <u>on</u> October 14.

I was born <u>on</u> June 22, 1968.

IN

LOCATION

Use *in* when something is inside another thing.

The books are <u>in</u> the big box.

I left my jacket <u>in</u> your car.

Barbara lives <u>in</u> Calgary.

TIME

Use *in* for a specific period of time, specific years, or for future appointments.

I am going to graduate from college <u>in</u> three years.

My best friend got married <u>in</u> 1994.

Mr. Johnson always drinks four cups of coffee <u>in</u> the morning.

We'll meet you <u>in</u> ten minutes.

MORE PREPOSITIONS

Here are a few more common prepositions. Remember that a preposition is always followed by a noun (or pronoun).

    with   to   for   by   near   under   from

Examples:

I am going <u>to</u> France <u>with</u> my cousin.

Marta bought a gift <u>for</u> her grandmother.

Please put that box <u>by</u> the door.

The student union is <u>near</u> my dorm.

Pedro keeps his shoes <u>under</u> his bed.

Did you get a job offer <u>from</u> that company?

Appendix 11

Some Common Comma Rules

1. Put a comma before *and, but, for, or, nor, so, yet,* when they connect two independent clauses.

   Richard bought Julie a candy bar, but he ate it himself.

2. Put a comma between three or more items in a series .

   Jennifer brought a towel, an umbrella, some sunscreen, and a book to the beach.

3. Put a comma after a clause with a connecting word when that clause begins a sentence.

   Because it was raining outside, Alex used his umbrella.

4. Put a comma before or after the name of a person spoken to.

   "Hamad, do you want to play soccer?" Ana asked.

   "Do you want to play soccer, Hamad?" Ana asked.

5. Commas separate parts of dates and places. Put a comma between the day and the date. Put a comma between the date and the year. Put a comma between a city and a state or a country.

   I was born on Wednesday, June 27, 1989.

   The concert was in Boston, Massachusetts.

   The headquarters of that company is located in Osaka, Japan.

Appendix 12

Order of Adjectives

Adjectives can go before nouns.

> He has a <u>white</u> car. It is a <u>new</u> car.

When more than one adjective is used before a noun, there is a certain order for the adjectives.

> *Incorrect:*   He has a white new car.
>
> *Correct:*   He has a new white car.

In general, there are seven kinds of adjectives, used in this order:

1. opinion   *beautiful, nice, ugly*
2. size   *small, large, huge*
3. shape   *round, square, oval*
4. condition   *broken, damaged, burned*
5. age   *old, young, new*
6. color   *red, white, green*
7. origin   *French, American, Korean*

It is common to have two adjectives before a noun and rare to have three or more adjectives before a noun. When there is more than one adjective before a noun, follow the order above. The noun always goes last. Remember that this list is only a general guideline.

> *Incorrect:*   a white small Japanese truck
>
> *Correct:*   a small white Japanese truck
>
> *Incorrect:*   a broken large dish
>
> *Correct:*   a large broken dish

Appendix 13

Definitions of Useful Language Terms

Adjective   A word that describes a noun.

Lexi is a very <u>smart</u> girl.

Adverb   A word that describes a verb or an adjective.

The secretary types <u>quickly</u>.

Article   The definite article is *the*. The indefinite articles are *a* and *an*.

<u>The</u> teacher gave <u>an</u> assignment to <u>the</u> students.

Jillian is eating <u>a</u> piece of cake.

Clause   A group of words that has a subject and a verb. Sentences can have one or more clauses.

<u>Roger</u> <u>wants</u> to go to Harvard University. (one clause)
SUBJECT VERB

<u>Jeff</u> <u>needs</u> to write his report because <u>he</u> <u>wants</u> to pass the class.
SUBJ. VERB   SUBJ. VERB
(CLAUSE 1)   (CLAUSE 2)

Noun   A noun is a person, place, thing, or idea.

<u>Sandra</u> likes to eat <u>sandwiches</u> for <u>lunch</u>.

<u>Love</u> is a very strong <u>emotion</u>.

Object   A word that comes after a transitive verb or a preposition.

Jim bought a new <u>car</u>.

I left my jacket in the <u>house</u>.

Predicate   The part of the sentence that shows what the subject does.

<u>Mr. Johnston</u> <u>walked to the park</u>.
SUBJECT   PREDICATE

<u>My neighbor's dog</u> <u>buried a bone in the yard</u>.
SUBJECT   PREDICATE

206

Preposition   A word that can show location, time, and direction. Some common prepositions are *around, at, behind, between, from, on, in, near, to, over, under, with.*

Punctuation   Punctuation includes the period (.), comma (,), question mark (?), and exclamation point (!).

Subject   The subject of a sentence tells who or what the sentence is about.

<u>My science teacher</u> gave us a homework assignment. <u>It</u> was difficult.

Tense   A verb has tense. Tense shows when the action happened.

Simple present:	She <u>walks</u> to school every day.
Present progressive:	She <u>is walking</u> to school now.
Simple past:	She <u>walked</u> to school yesterday.
Past progressive:	She <u>was walking</u> to school when she saw her friend.
Future:	She <u>is going to walk</u> to school.

Verb   The word that shows the action of the sentence.

They <u>speak</u> French.

My father <u>works</u> at the power plant.

Appendix 14

Extra Writing Activities for More Practice

Writing Activity 1 | **Writing a Paragraph (Unit 2)**

Read the paragraph and follow the steps below to create a new paragraph. Write the new paragraph on the lines provided. Be sure to write a new title for your paragraph.

EXAMPLE PARAGRAPH

California

[1]California is a large state. [2]It is located in the western part of the United States. [3]The population of California is approximately 33 million. [4]The largest cities in California are Los Angeles and San Francisco. [5]Millions of tourists visit this state every year. [6]They come for the beaches, the mountains, and the cities.

1. In sentences 1, 3, and 4, change *California* to *Florida*. Do the same for the title.

2. In sentence 2, change *western* to *southeastern*.

3. In sentence 3, change the population number from *33 million* to *15 million*.

4. In sentence 4, change the names of the cities from *Los Angeles and San Francisco* to *Miami, Tampa, and Orlando*.

5. In sentence 6, change *mountains* to *parks*.

6. In sentence 6, change *cities* to *great weather*.

_____

_____

_____

_____

_____

_____

_____

_____

| **Writing Activity 2** | **Writing a Paragraph (Unit 2)** |

Read the paragraph and follow the steps below to create a new paragraph. Write the new paragraph on the lines provided. Be sure to write a new title for your paragraph.

My Older Sister

EXAMPLE PARAGRAPH

¹I'd like to tell you about my older sister. ²Her name is Natalie. ³She is 26 years old. ⁴She is an elementary school teacher. ⁵She loves children. ⁶She is very patient and kind. ⁷My sister Natalie is a wonderful person.

1. In sentences 1 and 7, change *sister* to *brother*. Do the same for the title.
2. In sentences 3, 4, 5, and 6, change *she* to *he*.
3. In sentence 2, change *her* to *his*. Be sure to use a capital letter.
4. Natalie is a girl's name. In sentence 2, change *Natalie* to a boy's name of your choice.
5. In sentence 7, change *wonderful* to *great*.

_____

_____

_____

_____

_____

_____

_____

_____

Copyright © Houghton Mifflin Company. All rights reserved.

Writing Activity 3 — Writing a Paragraph (Unit 2)

Read the paragraph and follow the steps below to create a new paragraph. Write the new paragraph on the lines provided. Be sure to write a new title for your paragraph.

EXAMPLE PARAGRAPH

My House

¹I live in a small house. ²It is located on Princeton Street. ³My house number is 915. ⁴My house is new. ⁵It is two years old. ⁶The sides of my house are light yellow. ⁷The roof is light gray. ⁸In front of the house, there are many flowers. ⁹I am so lucky to live in this house!

1. In sentence 1, change *small* to *little*.
2. In sentence 2, change the name of street from *Princeton Street* to *Hillside Road*.
3. In sentence 3, change the house number from *915* to *710*.
4. In sentence 4, change *new* to *very old*.
5. In sentence 5, change the number *two* to an appropriate number for a very old house.
6. In sentences 6 and 7, change the color of the side of the house from *light yellow* to *white*. Change the color of the roof from *light gray* to *dark gray*.
7. In sentence 8, change the phrase *many flowers* to *some small bushes and trees*.

_____

_____

_____

_____

_____

_____

_____

_____

Writing Activity 4 — Write a Paragraph (Unit 2)

Read the paragraph and follow the steps below to create a new paragraph. Write the new paragraph on the lines provided. Be sure to write a new title for your paragraph.

EXAMPLE PARAGRAPH

A Desert Plant

¹The cactus is an interesting plant. ²It grows in the desert. ³It likes very hot temperatures. ⁴It does not need a lot of water to live. ⁵Its leaves are spiky. ⁶Many people grow this plant in their gardens.

1. In sentence 1, change *the cactus* to *seaweed*.
2. In sentence 2, change *desert* to *ocean*. Do the same in the title.
3. In sentence 3, make the verb *likes* negative.
4. In sentence 4, make the verb *does not need* affirmative.
5. In sentence 5, change *spiky* to *long and thin*.
6. In sentence 6, change *gardens* to *aquariums*.

_____

_____

_____

_____

_____

_____

_____

_____

_____

| **Writing Activity 5** | **Changing Proper Nouns to Subject Pronouns (Unit 2)** |

Fill in each blank with the correct subject pronoun (they, she, he, or it) for the proper noun in parentheses ( ). Then copy the new paragraph on the lines below. Give the paragraph a title.

Susan Brown and Joey Chen are actors. (**1.** Joey and Susan) _____ have very

interesting careers. Susan acts in plays in the theater. (**2.** Susan) _____ works in

New York City. (**3.** New York City) _____ is the best place to work in the theater.

Joey acts in movies. (**4.** Joey) _____ works in Los Angeles. (**5.** Los Angeles)

_____ is an exciting city. (**6.** People) _____ make lots of movies there.

Joey and Susan are very happy with their jobs. (**7.** Joey and Susan) _____ would

not do anything else.

_____

_____

_____

_____

_____

_____

_____

_____

_____

_____

| Writing Activity 6 | **Changing Nouns to Object Pronouns (Unit 3)** |

Read the paragraph and follow the steps below to create a new paragraph. Write the new paragraph on the lines provided. Be sure to write a title for your paragraph.

EXAMPLE PARAGRAPH

¹Last week Jane and I moved into a new apartment. ²We were very excited. ³We moved many big things into (our new apartment). ⁴I had a television. ⁵We put (the television) in the living room next to the window. ⁶Jane's brother helped (Jane and me) move our couch and chairs. ⁷We told (Jane's brother) to put (the couch and chairs) in front of the television. ⁸Finally, we moved in our beds. ⁹It took a long time to bring (the beds) in. ¹⁰Jane said she would move her bed alone, but her brother had to help (Jane). ¹¹Moving is a lot of hard work. I hope we don't have to move again soon!

1. Change all the words in parentheses into an object pronoun (*me, her, him, us, them, it*).

2. In sentence 9, make the verb negative.

3. In sentence 10, change the word *alone* to the phrase *by herself*.

_____

_____

_____

_____

_____

_____

_____

_____

_____

_____

_____

| **Writing Activity 7** | **Past Tense Verbs (Unit 4)** |

Read the paragraph and follow the steps below to create a new paragraph. Write the new paragraph on the lines provided.

EXAMPLE PARAGRAPH

Life on the Farm

¹My grandpa is a very busy farmer. ²Every day he gets up at four o'clock in the morning. ³He eats breakfast. ⁴Then he goes out to the barn. ⁵There he feeds and milks the cows. ⁶When he finishes, he feeds the rest of the animals. ⁷Then he works in the cornfields until noon. ⁸He eats a fast lunch. ⁹After that, he works in the fields again. ¹⁰In the evening, he eats dinner. ¹¹Then he feeds the animals one last time. ¹²Grandpa finally goes to bed at around nine o'clock. ¹³He certainly does a lot in one day!

1. In sentence 2, change *every day* to *yesterday*.
2. In sentences 2–13, change all the verbs to past tense. Be careful of irregular verbs!

Life on the Farm

_____

_____

_____

_____

_____

_____

_____

_____

| **Writing Activity 8** | **Sentence Combining (Unit 4)** |

Read the paragraph. It is missing three sentences. Combine the sentences that follow the paragraph.
Use and, but, *or* so. *Then write the three new sentences in the correct place in the paragraph.*

Lars's New Career

Lars is studying nursing. (**1.**) _____

_____

Lars also practices nursing at a local hospital. (**2.**) _____

_____

He is not ready to do that yet. (**3.**) _____

_____ Because of this, it will be easy for him to get a

good job. Then he can help as many people as possible.

Missing sentence 1:	He has to go to school every day.
	He takes several classes every day.
Missing sentence 2:	He helps with everyday work there.
	He cannot help with emergencies.
Missing sentence 3:	Lars's grades are very good.
	He will graduate with honors.

| Writing Activity 9 | Changing Past Tense to Future Tense (Unit 6) |

Read the paragraph and follow the steps below to create a new paragraph. Write the new paragraph on the lines provided.

EXAMPLE PARAGRAPH

A Memorable Vacation

¹When I was thirteen years old, my aunt and uncle took me on a wonderful vacation. ²We went to the Black Hills in South Dakota. ³We did lots of interesting things. ⁴We visited Mt. Rushmore and took lots of pictures. ⁵We visited a place to mine for gold. ⁶One night, we even ate buffalo burgers for dinner. ⁷It was very exciting. ⁸I made memories on that trip that I will keep for a lifetime.

1. In sentence 1, change *When I was thirteen years old* to *When I graduate from high school this year.*
2. Change all the verbs in the paragraph to *be going to* + verb.

A Memorable Vacation

_____
_____
_____
_____
_____
_____
_____
_____
_____

| Writing Activity 10 | Adjective Clauses (Unit 7) |

Read the paragraph below. Three pairs of sentences are underlined. Combine each pair of sentences by using an adjective clause. Rewrite the paragraph with your new sentences on the lines provided. The first pair of sentences has been done for you.

EXAMPLE PARAGRAPH

The Discovery of the *Titanic*

[1]There were many scientists and explorers. They searched for the *Titanic* for a long time. They finally found it in 1985. It was deep in the Atlantic Ocean. This water was too deep for humans to visit without protection. Scientists solved this problem. [2]In order to explore the wreck, they used a **submersible**. This submersible was **controlled** by people on the surface of the ocean. Explorers took pictures of the *Titanic* with the submersible. [3]They even brought things to the surface. These things were on the **sunken** ship. Because of these people's efforts, we now understand more about the remains of the *Titanic*.

submersible: a vehicle that can go very deep underwater

control: to guide

sunken: covered by water

The Discovery of the *Titanic*

There were many scientists and explorers who searched for the *Titanic* for a long time.

_____

_____

_____

_____

_____

_____

Appendix 15

Peer Editing Sheets

PEER EDITING SHEET #1   **UNIT 1, Activity 18, page 26**

Writer: _____ Date: _____

Peer editor: _____

1. In three or four words, what is the topic? (What did the writer write about?) _____

   _____

2. How many sentences did the writer write? _____

3. Does each sentence begin with a capital letter? _____ If not, which sentences need to be fixed?

   _____

4. Does each sentence have a period or question mark at the end? _____ If not, which sentences

   need to be fixed? _____

5. What is the longest sentence? _____ How many words does it have? _____

6. Do you see an error in any sentences? If so, write one sentence with a correction here:

   _____

   _____

PEER EDITING SHEET #2   **UNIT 2, Activity 18, page 57**

Writer: _____ Date: _____

Peer editor: _____

1. Where does your partner want to go? _____

2. What is one reason that your partner wants to visit this place? _____

    _____

    _____

3. How many sentences are in your partner's paragraph? _____

4. Did your partner remember to indent the first line of the paragraph? _____

5. Does the paragraph have a topic sentence? _____

6. Write the topic sentence here: _____

    _____

7. Does the paragraph contain any adjectives? If so, write them here. _____

    _____

8. Do you have any questions about what your partner wrote? (Are there any unclear sentences?) If

    so, write your questions here. _____

    _____

    _____

    _____

PEER EDITING SHEET #3   **UNIT 3, Activity 16, page 76**

Writer: _____ Date: _____

Peer editor: _____

1. What sport did the writer choose to write about? _____

2. Did you know about this sport before you read this paragraph? _____

3. Does the paragraph have a topic sentence? _____ If so, write it here. _____

   _____

   _____

4. How many sentences are in the paragraph? _____

5. Does each sentence begin with a capital letter? _____ If not, write the sentences that need to

   be fixed here. _____

   _____

6. Does each sentence have a period or question mark at the end? _____ If not, write the sen-

   tences that need to be fixed here. _____

   _____

7. Which sentence has the most adjectives in it? Write the sentence here and circle the adjectives.

   _____

   _____

8. Does every sentence have a verb? _____ If not, copy one of the sentences that is missing a

   verb here and add a correct verb. _____

   _____

9. If there is a compound sentence in the paragraph, write it here. Circle the connecting word.

_____

_____

10. Did the writer use any object pronouns? If so, write a sentence that contains one here. Circle the

object pronoun. _____

_____

11. Write another sentence about the topic here. (Write your own original sentence.)

_____

_____

PEER EDITING SHEET #4   **UNIT 4, Activity 17, page 98**

Writer: _____ Date: _____

Peer editor: _____

1. Who did your partner write about? _____

2. Why do you think the writer chose this person? _____
    _____

3. Can you find a sentence that tells where the person lived? _____

4. Copy the topic sentence here: _____
    _____
    _____

5. Now circle the subject in the topic sentence. Underline the verb.

6. How many sentences are there? _____ How many verbs are there? _____

7. In general, it is not good to have the same number of verbs and sentences. If these two numbers
    are the same, this means that the writer uses subject-verb order and simple sentences too often.
    The writer needs to work on sentence variety. Suggest that the writer try to combine sentences.

8. Write a few of the past tense verbs here. _____

9. How many times can you find *was*? _____ *were*? _____ Irregular past verbs? _____
    Past negative verbs? _____

10. Are there any compound sentences that use *but*? _____ If not, suggest two sentences that can
    be connected with *but*. Write them here.
    _____

_____

11. Did the writer use any time phrases? If so, write them here. _____

_____

12. Is there an additional piece of information about the person that you would like to know? Write a

question about this information. _____

_____

Writer: _____ Date: _____

Peer editor: _____

1. Is the first line of the paragraph indented? _____

2. How many *-ing* verbs can you find in the paragraph? _____

3. Can you find a sentence that has *and* or *so* as a connector? Write it here.

   _____

   _____

4. Does every sentence have a subject and a verb? _____ If not, copy one of the incorrect sen-

   tences here. Then correct it. _____

   _____

   _____

5. Adjectives help make writing easy to see or imagine. Can you find a sentence that does not have
   any adjectives? Copy it here and add two adjectives. Circle the two adjectives that you added.

   _____

   _____

   _____

6. Does the paragraph have any sentences that contain adverbs of manner? If yes, copy one of them here.

   _____

   _____

   _____

7. Can you find any spelling mistakes? _____ Write the misspelled word and its correct spelling below.

Misspelled word   Correctly spelled word

a. _____   a. _____

b. _____   b. _____

c. _____   c. _____

d. _____   d. _____

8. Do you have any comments or suggestions for the writer? If so, write them here.

_____

_____

PEER EDITING SHEET #6   **UNIT 6, Activity 16, page 143**

Writer: _____ Date: _____

Peer editor: _____

1. What event does the writer describe in this paragraph? _____

    _____

    _____

2. Check for these features: a. _____ Is there a topic sentence?

                               b. _____ Do all the sentences relate to one topic?

                               c. _____ Is the first line indented?

3. What is the topic sentence? Copy it here. _____

    _____

    _____

4. Check for mistakes with subject-verb agreement. If the subject is singular, is the verb singular, too? If the subject is plural, is the verb plural, too? If you find any mistakes, circle them.

5. Is it easy for you to understand the meaning of the sentences in this paragraph? _____

    If not, copy a sentence that is hard for you to understand clearly. _____

    _____

6. Does the writer have articles in every place where they are needed? _____ If not, add

    them in the paper.

7. Do you have any ideas or suggestions for improving the paragraph? _____

    _____

    _____

Writer: _____ Date: _____

Peer editor: _____

1. What is the writer's opinion about cooking food at home or eating in a restaurant? Check one.

    _____ Cooking food at home is better.

    _____ Eating in a restaurant is better.

    _____ Both options are about the same.

2. What is one reason that the writer thinks that choice is better? _____

    _____

3. Copy the sentence here that tells you the answer to number 2. _____

    _____

    _____

4. Does the sentence in number 3 have a subject and a verb? _____ If yes, underline the subject one time and the verb two times. If not, add the missing words.

5. Is the first line indented? _____ If not, put an arrow to show that the line needs to be indented.

6. Does the paragraph have a complex sentence? _____ If yes, write it below. If not, make a suggestion about combining two simple sentences from the paragraph. _____

    _____

    _____

7. Do you think this paragraph is too long, too short, or just right? _____

8. Does the writer include adjective clauses in the paragraph? Write the clauses below.

_____

_____

9. Do you have any suggestions for making this paragraph better? _____

_____

_____

_____

Writer: _____ Date: _____

Peer editor: _____

1. What is the writer's opinion about smoking in restaurants and bars? _____

   _____

   _____

   _____

2. Do you agree with the writer's opinion? _____

3. Explain your answer in number 2. _____

   _____

   _____

   _____

   _____

4. Check for these features: a. _____ Is there a topic sentence?

   b. _____ Do all the sentences relate to one topic?

   c. _____ Is the first line indented?

5. What is the topic sentence? Copy it here. _____

   _____

   _____

6. Are articles used correctly? Circle any errors with articles.

7. Was it easy for you to understand the language in the paragraph? _____ If not, copy one of the

confusing parts (sentences) here. _____

_____

_____

_____

8. How many sentences does this paragraph have? _____ How many sentences do *not* have a

verb? _____

9. Can you think of anything to make this a better paragraph? _____

_____

_____

_____

_____

Writer: _____ Date: _____

Peer editor: _____

1. What is the writer's opinion about what to do in this case? _____

   _____

   _____

   _____

   _____

2. Do you agree or disagree with the writer's ideas? _____

3. Please explain your answer to number 2. _____

   _____

   _____

   _____

   _____

4. Are all the verbs in the correct tense? If not, write a sentence here with an incorrect verb. Then

   make the correction.

   _____

   _____

5. Does every sentence end in the correct punctuation? _____ If not, put a circle around the

   place where the punctuation should go.

6. Can you understand everything the writer wanted to say? _____ If not, write one of the

unclear parts here. _____

_____

_____

Why is this unclear to you? _____

_____

_____

7. Can you add two or more interesting adjectives in front of two nouns? (Add them on the student's

paper. Draw an arrow to show where they should go.) What are your two adjectives? Use Appendix

12 if you need help with the correct order. _____

_____

Appendix 16

Answer Key

UNIT 1

p. 3, gato = Spanish, te rog = Romanian, shukran = Arabic, tomber = French, samui = Japanese, sedap = Malay, chang-moon = Korean

p. 4, Ci sono dodici studenti nella classe. = Italian; 這位學生是來自加拿大。 = Chinese; Miklós beszél franciául és angolul. = Hungarian; Pisica are o coadă și patru picioare. = Romanian

Activity 1, p. 5 2. There are only four people. 3. I have two parents. 4. José is my father's name. (OR My father's name is José.) 5. My mother's name is Karina. (OR Karina is my mother's name.) 6. I have one brother. 7. His name is Andy. 8. I love my family very much.

Activity 2, p. 5 Answers will vary.

Activity 3, p. 7 1. Most kids like spaghetti. 2. They enjoy the taste of spaghetti. 3. They love the smell of spaghetti. 4. Some kids put tomato sauce on their spaghetti. 5. Other kids like cheese on their spaghetti.

Activity 4, p. 8 Answers will vary.

Activity 5, pp. 8–9 2. His name is Albert. 3. Albert is a taxi driver. 4. He is a good taxi driver. 5. Albert works for a large taxi company. 6. The name of the taxi company is Lightning Taxi Service. 7. Albert drives a taxi six days a week. 8. He meets interesting people from many different places.

Activity 6, pp. 11–12 2. What city is the White House in? The White House is in Washington, D.C. 3. What country is the Nile River in? The Nile River is in Egypt. 4. What city is the Eiffel Tower in? The Eiffel Tower is in Paris. 5. What is the biggest city in Mexico? Mexico City is the biggest city in Mexico. 6. Where are the Andes Mountains? The Andes Mountains are in South America. 7. What is the capital of Saudi Arabia? Riyadh is the capital of Saudi Arabia. 8. What is the biggest province in Canada? Quebec is the biggest province in Canada.

Activity 7, pp. 12–13 3. S Some months have thirty days. 4. S An example of this is September. 5. S Other months have thirty-one days. 6. S Examples are July and December. 7. Q What month never has thirty days? 8. S The answer is February.

9. S February usually has twenty-eight days. 10. S Everyone in my family was born in February. (OR Everyone in my family was born in February!)

Activity 8, pp. 13–14 1. What is your name? 2. Where are you from? 3. Where do you live? 4. How many people are in your family? 5. Do you have a car? 6. What food do you like to eat? 7. What is your favorite place to visit? 8. What is your favorite movie? [Answers from classmates will vary.]

Activity 9, pp. 14–15 1. Where is Costa Rica? 2. Costa Rica is a country in Central America. 3. It is between Panama and Nicaragua. 4. It is between the Atlantic Ocean and the Pacific Ocean. 5. The population is approximately two million. 6. Many tourists go there. 7. They see wild animals in the jungle. 8. It is the most beautiful country in the world! 9. I want to visit this beautiful country. 10. Do you want to visit Costa Rica?

Activity 10, p. 16 Answers will vary.

Activity 11, p. 18 3. F 4. S 5. F 6. F 7. S 8. F 9. S 10. S

Activity 12, pp. 18–19 1. Tuna salad 2. The ingredients 3. Two ingredients 4. I 5. I 6. I 7. I 8. Tuna salad

Activity 13, p. 19

Tuna salad is easy to make. The ingredients are simple and cheap. Two ingredients are tuna fish and mayonnaise. I also use onions, salt, and pepper. First, I cut up the onions. Then I add the tuna fish and the mayonnaise. Finally, I add some salt and a lot of pepper. Tuna salad is my favorite food!

Activity 14, p. 20 1. Caroline Jimenez works . . . 2. She works . . . 3. . . . she attends . . . 4. Caroline wakes up . . . 5. She starts . . . 6. She works . . . 7. Her lunch break is . . . 8. Caroline likes . . . 9. She enjoys . . . 10. She loves . . . 10. Anderson Supermarket is . . .

Activity 15, pp. 21–22 1. X incorrect capitalization. Burundi is in Africa. 2. X missing verb *be*. Canada is bigger than the United States. 3. X incorrect punctuation. A popular city in Florida is Miami. 4. C 5. X subject missing. He visits the Mayan ruins in Central America every year! 6. X verb missing. Bolivia has no seaports. 7. C 8. X missing verb *be*. Austria and Hungary are in Europe. 9. X subject missing. The United States is between Mexico and Canada. 10. X subject missing. The population of Thailand is about 30,000,000.

Activity 16, pp. 22–23 Tuscany *is* a beautiful region in Italy. *It* is famous for cities such as *F*lorence, Siena, and Pisa. The *A*ppenine Hills *are* in Tuscany. Tuscany *is* also famous for wine making. For example, Chianti and Montalcino wines *are* very popular and tasty. Tuscany has so many interesting places to see. *It* is a wonderful place to visit!

Activity 17, pp. 23–25 Answers will vary.

UNIT 2

Activity 1, pp. 31–32 2. I don't like this humid weather. 3. Paris is a beautiful city in France. 4. Ali has a part-time job. 5. They like to drink diet cola. 6. Marian reads international folk tales. 7. My mother grows big beautiful roses. 8. Gillian works for a small, independent company. 9. My grandparents live in a small farming town. 10. Sharon rents a tiny gray house on Smith Street.

Activity 2, p. 33 I have a dream to visit Alaska. The weather is <u>beautiful</u> there. I love <u>cold</u> weather. When the temperature is <u>low</u>, I have energy! I also want to visit Alaska because I love nature. Alaska is <u>pure</u> and <u>natural</u>. I dream about the <u>beautiful</u> landscape. In addition, there are <u>wild</u> animals. Finally, I want to learn <u>important</u> information about the <u>native</u> people of Alaska. I hope to visit <u>beautiful</u> Alaska soon.

Activity 3, pp. 34–37 Paragraph 5: 1. 6 2. (b) 3. My favorite color is blue. 4. b. The writer wears blue jeans almost every day. c. The writer has a pair of light blue tennis shoes. d. The writer owns a blue car. e. The writer's computer is blue. OR The writer has a blue computer. 5. Other colors are nice, but I like blue the best. 6. favorite, six, blue, blue, every, light, blue, tennis, blue, other, nice. Paragraph 6: 1. 9 2. (c) 3. I work in an interesting building. 4. a. The building is in downtown Atlanta. b. The name of the building is the Franklin Building. c. The building is dark red. d. The building has six floors. 5. Everyone likes the Franklin Building very much. 6. interesting, downtown, dark, many, six, each, different.

Activity 4, pp. 38–39

Paragraph 7:

Most kids like spaghetti. They enjoy the taste of spaghetti. They love the smell of spaghetti. Some kids put tomato sauce on their spaghetti. Other kids like cheese on their spaghetti.

Title: Answers will vary. **Topic sentence:** <u>Most kids like spaghetti.</u>

Paragraph 8:

This is my cousin. His name is Albert. Albert is a taxi driver. He is a good taxi driver. Albert works for a large taxi company. The name of the taxi company is Lightning Taxi Service. Albert drives a taxi six days a week. He meets interesting people from many different places.

Title: Answers will vary. **Topic sentence:** <u>This is my cousin.</u>

Activity 5, p. 40 Answers will vary.

Activity 6, pp. 41–42

Paragraph 9: a. My cousin Maria is an excellent server. Paragraph 10: c. My favorite city in the world is New York City. Paragraph 11: b. Some people like snow, but I don't.

Activity 7, pp. 42–43

Paragraph 12: c. Pasta is my favorite food. Paragraph 13: b. Good teachers have special qualities. Paragraph 14: a. This city offers radio stations for everyone.

Activity 8, p. 44 2. He 3. They 4. It 5. It 6. They 7. they 8. It

Activity 9, pp. 46–48

Paragraph 16:

(Keeping score in American football is more difficult than keeping score in soccer.)

Another sport that has easy scoring is basketball.

Paragraph 17:

(Changing temperatures from Celsius to Fahrenheit is not difficult.) Many countries

report temperatures in Celsius, but the United States uses Fahrenheit.

Paragraph 18:

(Chili is an easy and delicious dish to prepare.) Fried chicken is also easy to prepare.

Activity 10, p. 48 2. their 3. Her 4. her 5. Their 6. Their 7. His 8. her
Activity 11, p. 49 1. my 2. my 3. Her 4. Her 5. She 6. She 7. She 8. her 9. She
   10. Their 11. My 12. Their 13. I 14. my 15. they 16. my

Activity 12, pp. 49–50

Paragraph 21: Arizona is also in the Southwest. There are no states that begin with the
   word "Old." Paragraph 22: My grandmother lived to be 87. She does not like to
   cook rice. Paragraph 23: My father makes bookcases and other wood furniture. I
   have trouble remembering my telephone number.

Activity 13, p. 51 The best types of food *are* . . . It *is* important . . . . . . exercise *is* good
   . . . relaxation *is* very important.

Activity 14, pp. 52–53

Paragraph 9: Topic sentence: My cousin Maria is an excellent server. Concluding sentence: Maria wants every customer to have a good meal at the restaurant.

Paragraph 10: Topic sentence: My favorite city in the world is New York City.
   Concluding sentence: I truly enjoy New York City.

Paragraph 11: Topic sentence: Some people like the snow, but I don't. Concluding sentence: I understand why some people like snow, but I don't like it very much.

Paragraph 12: Topic sentence: Pasta is my favorite food. Concluding sentence: I want to
   eat pasta every day!

Paragraph 13: Topic sentence: Good teachers have special qualities. Concluding sentence: These are some of the most important qualities of good teachers.

Paragraph 14: Topic sentence: This city offers radio stations for everyone. Concluding
   sentence: This city is lucky to have so many kinds of music stations.

Activity 15, pp. 53–54

Paragraph 25: c. These are just a few reasons why I don't like Monday.

Paragraph 26: b. Many people believe in good and bad superstitions.

Paragraph 27: a. It is important to think about these things when you are buying a car.

Activity 16, p. 54

Aspirin is an incredible medicine. This small white drug ***is an old medicine***. We do not know exactly why or how it works. However, millions of people use aspirin every day. **W**e take aspirin for ***many reasons***. Aspirin ***is*** good for headaches, colds, and pain. Aspirin can help with so many different health problems. Aspirin is a ***simple medicine***, but it ***is*** great.

Activity 17, pp. 55–56 Answers will vary.

UNIT 3

Activity 1, p. 63 1. is 2. is 3. has 4. works 5. go 6. love 7. Do you know

Activity 2, p. 63 1. is 2. are 3. is 4. are 5. are 6. am / 'm 7. are 8. are

Activity 3, p. 64

Jim and Billy are very busy students. They study engineering at City College. Every day they wake up at 7:00 in the morning, take a shower, and then rush off to school. They go to school for six hours. After school, they go to the local mall where they work in a sporting goods store. After this part-time job, they go home, eat a quick dinner, study, and do their homework. Jim and Billy know that this lifestyle is stressful. They also know that it will end soon, and they will get a professional job.

Activity 4, p. 64–66 Answers may vary. 1. makes breakfast 2. sits down at the kitchen table 3. read the newspaper 4. looks at his watch and motions for the kids to get their lunch boxes 5. say goodbye 6. get into 7. Mrs. Lee rinses the breakfast dishes at the sink. 8. Mrs. Lee gets into her car to go to work.

Activity 5, pp. 66–67

Budapest ***is*** one of the most interesting capitals of Europe. ***It*** is a romantic city, and it has many interesting tourist places to visit. One example ***is*** the Danube River. It separates Budapest into Buda and Pest. In addition, visitors ***love*** Hungarian traditional food. The most popular food ***is*** goulash soup. The people of Budapest ***are*** friendly and helpful to tourists. When ***you*** travel to Europe, you can visit Budapest and have a very good time.

Activity 6, p. 67

Do you know about the TOEFL? It is the Test of English as a Foreign Language. Most international students who want to study at a university in the **U**nited **S**tates take this test. **I**t measures **E**nglish language ability. The test comes from Educational Testing Service in **N**ew **J**ersey. It is a very long test. **T**he computer version of the TOEFL contains four tasks: Listening Comprehension, Structure, Reading Comprehension, and Essay Writing. **I**f you want to study in the **U**nited **S**tates, it is important to prepare for this test and get a high score.

Activity 7, p. 68 2. is not/isn't 3. is not/isn't 4. does not/doesn't 5. are not/aren't 6. are not/aren't 7. does not/doesn't 8. is not/isn't 9. does not/doesn't 10. does not/doesn't

Activity 8, p. 69 1. her 2. them 3. it 4. them 5. her 6. us

Activity 9, p. 70 Answers will vary.

Activity 10, pp. 70–71 Answers will vary.

Activity 11, p. 72 3. C 4. S 5. S 6. S 7. C 8. S 9. S 10. C 11. C 12. S

Activity 12, pp. 72–73 1. Mary lives in Turkey, but Abdul lives in Kuwait. 2. The weather was cold, so I stayed indoors. 3. We go to school every day, and we play tennis on weekends. 4. Linus and Kathy are related, but they are not brother and sister. 5. The restaurant manager was happy, so he gave all the servers a raise.

Writer's Note, pp. 73–74 11 and 12: Answers will vary.

Activity 13, pp. 74–75 What is a popular sport? Where did this sport come from? (What is the history of this sport?) Is soccer an international sport? Where (in which countries) is this sport popular? Why is it popular? What special equipment does this sport require? Is this sport popular on television? Is there a worldwide competition in this sport? How often is it played? How do soccer fans feel about this competition?

Activity 14, p. 75 Steven Mills is not a typical teenager. Steven is a gymnast, and he wan*ts* to compete in the **O**lympics. He wakes up at five o'clock in the morning every day. He has a ***healthy breakfast***. Then **h**e jogs to National Gymnasium on **C**ypress Street He practices gymnastics for two hours. Then he gets ready for school. Steven goes to school from eight-thirty in the morning until three o'clock in the afternoon. After school, he returns to the gymnasium for ***special classes*** with **his** coach. When practice finish**es** at six o'clock, Steven returns home. He eats dinner, does his homework, and talks with **his** family. Steven is in bed by ten o'clock, so he will be ready for work the next day.

Activity 15, p. 76 Answers will vary.

UNIT 4

Activity 1, pp. 80–81 2. Mary and Natalie petted many animals. 3. They laughed at the animals. 4. Natalie really enjoyed herself. 5. She liked the chickens best. 6. Natalie watched them play all morning. 7. They played with the baby goats. 8. Finally, they returned home.

Activity 2, pp. 81–82

Lao-Tzu (was) a Chinese philosopher. He (was) born in China. He (lived) in the Hunan province. Lao-Tzu (worked) as a court librarian. The government (was) corrupt. Lao-Tzo (decided) to leave his home. Before he (abandoned) the province, someone (asked) him to write a book about how to live correctly. He (agreed) to write the book *Tao Te Ching*. It (was) the beginning of the philosophy of Taoism.

2. He was born in China. 3. He was a court librarian. 4. He agreed to write the book *Tao Te Ching*. 5. This book created the philosophy of Taoism.

Activity 3, p. 82 Answers will vary.

Activity 4, pp. 82–83

In 1992, Anthony and Marcus ⟨were⟩ students at the University of North Carolina. They ⟨were⟩ in the criminology department. They ⟨were⟩ excellent in their studies. In class, they ⟨answered⟩ all of their instructors' questions. Their test grades ⟨were⟩ the best, and their class projects ⟨were⟩ excellent. When they graduated in 1996, they ⟨finished⟩ at the top of the class. The teachers ⟨were⟩ very proud of Anthony and Marcus.

In 1992, Marcia was a student at the University of North Carolina. She was in the criminology department. She was excellent in her studies. In class, she answered all of her instructors' questions. Her test grades were the best, and her class projects were excellent. When she graduated in 1996, she finished at the top of the class.

The teachers were very proud of Marcia.

Activity 5, pp. 84–85 Answers may vary. 2. She was from the United States (America). 3. She was healthy when she was born. Or: She was born healthy. 4. She became ill when she was two years old. 5. Her teacher was Annie Sullivan. 6. Helen Keller was seven years old when she learned to communicate. 7. Helen was twenty years old when she started college. 8. She wrote thirteen books and traveled around the world.

Activity 6, pp. 86–87 1 and 2 Answers will vary.

Activity 7, p. 87 Answers will vary.

Activity 8, pp. 88–89 2. was not 3. was 4. was 5. were not 6. were 7. were 8. was 9. were 10. were not 11. were not

Activity 9, pp. 89–90 2. Shelley did not/didn't study engineering. 3. Herbert's parents did not/ didn't visit him last year. 4. Dinosaurs did not/didn't have large brains. 5. John did not/didn't help me with my homework!

Activity 10, pp. 90–91 2. Confucius did not/didn't live in Japan. He lived in China. 3. Pele did not/didn't play basketball. He played soccer. 4. The Beatles did not/didn't sing in Arabic. They sang in English. 5. The *Titanic* did not/didn't sink in the Pacific Ocean. It sank in the Atlantic Ocean. 6. The Statue of Liberty did not/didn't come from Italy. It came from France. 7. Thomas Edison did not/didn't invent the radio. He invented the light bulb among other things. 8. Stephen King did not/didn't write *Romeo and Juliet*. He wrote *The Green Mile*. Shakespeare wrote *Romeo and Juliet*. 9. The prophet Mohammed did not/didn't speak Hindi. He spoke Arabic. 10. Marilyn Monroe was not/wasn't an engineer. She was an actress.

Activity 11, pp. 91–92 2. was 3. did not/didn't work 4. woke up 5. was 6. did not/didn't start 7. got 8. yelled 9. crashed 10. lost 11. stayed 12. decided 13. was

Activity 12, p. 93 4. C . . . decision, but . . . 5. S 6. C . . . Canada, but . . . 7. S 8. C . . . sports, but . . . 9. S 10. S 11. C . . . pine, but . . . 12. S

Activity 13, pp. 94–95 Answers may vary. 2. Andrew was born in 1915, but Ian was born in 1920. 3. Andrew sang as a hobby, but Ian played baseball. 4. Andrew was married, but Ian was single. 5. Andrew lived in Washington, D.C., but Ian lived in Chicago, Illinois. 6. Andrew graduated from high school, but Ian graduated from college with a bachelor's degree. 7. Andrew was a firefighter, but Ian was a high school math teacher. 8. Andrew died on March 23, 1985, but Ian died on September 12, 1992.

Activity 14, p. 95 Answers will vary.

Activity 15, p. 96

Ibn Batuta **was** a famous **M**oroccan traveler. He live**d** in Morocco in the fourteenth century. When he was a **young man**, he made a religious trip to Mecca. However, Ibn Batuta love**d** to see new places so much that he continued to travel. This was **not** his original plan, but he continued on his journey. He had many adventures during **his** travels, and he met many interesting people. After he returned home, he did not forg**e**t about his journey. He wrote a book about his travels. **T**his book now gives us a lot of **important information** about life in the fourteenth century. **It** also gives us more information about this interesting and important man.

Activity 16, p. 97 Answers will vary.

UNIT 5

Activity 1, p. 100 1. are visiting 2. are walking 3. are watching 4. are playing 5. are swinging 6. are having 7. is looking 8. is eating 9. is walking 10. are talking 11. is walking 12. is yawning 13. is talking 14. is telling 15. are listening 16. are asking

Activity 2, pp. 100–101 Answers may vary. 1. is vacuuming 2. is taking 3. is picking up 4. is washing the window

Activity 3, pp. 102–103 1. . . . is going into the net 2. . . . is jumping for the ball 3. . . . is watching the ball 4. . . . is running toward the goal 5. . . . hopes the shot will be a goal 6. . . . are cheering for their team 7. . . . are waving flags and banners

Activity 4, p. 103 Answers will vary.

Activity 5, p. 105 2. . . . vitamin C, and milk has . . . 3. . . . South America, and Switzerland is . . . 4. . . . for you, and they are . . . 5. . . . seeds, and I hope they . . .

Activity 6, p. 106 2. Dharma lives in a dormitory. Greta is her roommate. 3. Dharma is going to graduate at the end of the year. Greta is going to graduate at the end of the year. 4. Dharma wants to get a good job in the private sector when she graduates. Greta wants to get a good job in the private sector when she graduates. 5. Dharma hopes to work for Motorola. Greta wants to get a job with Florida Power & Light Company.

Activity 7, pp. 107–108 2. a) R b) C It rained really hard, so we didn't play tennis. 3. a) R b) C The cat was very sick, so we took it to the vet. 4. a) C b) R The audience loved the show, so they applauded wildly. 5. a) C b) R Jonathan didn't feel well, so he didn't go to the party. 6. a) R b) C The record was very expensive, so I didn't buy it. 7. a) C b) R The plane didn't leave on time, so we arrived at our destination late. 8. a) C b) R She forgot to set her alarm clock, so she woke up late.

Activity 8, pp. 108–111 Answers will vary. Here are some suggestions. 2. The boy wants to skate outside, so he is putting on his roller skates. 3. The dog is hungry, so it is howling. 4. The speaker is boring, so the two men are yawning. 5. The computer is not working properly, so the woman is frustrated. 6. The man is cooking, so he is using a lot of pots and pans.

Activity 9, p. 112 3. S 4. C . . . the question, so I will ask . . . 5. S 6. C . . . city, so you can't see . . . 7. S 8. C . . . *honesty*, and verbs . . . 9. C . . . IBM, but she . . . 10. S 11. C . . . Khartoum, and it is . . . 12. C . . . plane, so she . . .

Activity 10, p. 113 Answers will vary. Here are some possibilities. 1. quietly; hard 2. quickly 3. nervously; confidently 4. poorly 5. softly

Activity 11, p. 114 Answers will vary.

Activity 12, pp. 114–115

A small brown squirrel *is* climbing a tree. He looks like a young squirrel. His tail is twitching nervously**,** and his nose is moving *quickly*. I think he is looking for food. Now the *brown squirrel* is on a long tree branch. He wants to jump to another tree. The squirrel hears something**,** so he looks down. *H*e is coming down from the *green tree*. Someone dropped a few pieces of chocolate chip cookie. These pieces *are* lying on the grass. *T*he squirrel is walking toward the food, and he is inspecting it. He is putting it in his mouth. His tail is moving *rapidly*. The little brown squirrel is now eating happily.

Activity 13, pp. 115–116 Answers will vary.

UNIT 6

Activity 1, pp. 120–122 Answers may vary. Here are some possibilities. 1. It is/it's going to rain. 2. She is/She's going to get married. 3. He is/He's going to score a goal. 4. She is/She's going to start an experiment. 5. They are/They're going to go backpacking. 6. He is/He's going to fall off a chair.

Activity 2, p. 123 2. He is going to meet with Mr. Green. 3. He is going to have dinner with Andrea on Friday. 4. He is going to take his pet to the vet (veterinarian). 5. He is going to buy groceries. 6. He is going to play soccer on Saturday at 6 P.M. 7. He is going to give him a business report.

Activity 3, p. 124 Answers will vary.

Activity 4, pp. 125–126 1. First 2. Tuesday 3. next 4. After that 5. Finally

Activity 5, pp. 126–127 1. . . . is going to be 15 years old. 2. . . . is going to wear . . . 3. . . . is going to go . . . 4. . . . are going to go . . . 5. . . . are going to have . . . 6. . . . is going to perform . . . 7. . . . is going to dance 8. . . . (is going to) eat 9. . . . (is going to) celebrate. 10. . . . is never going to forget . . .

1. She/Carmen is going to be 15 years old. 2. She/Carmen is going to wear a beautiful white gown. 3. First, she/Carmen is going to go to church . . . 4. Carmen's/her *quince* party is going to be held in a beautiful ballroom. 5. She and her friends/They are/They're going to dance, eat, and celebrate.

Activity 6, p. 128 Answers will vary.

Activity 7, p. 130 4. CX 5. S 6. CD . . . next year, but her brother is going . . . 7. . . . is over, we're going to . . . 8. S 9. CD . . . are sisters, but they don't get along . . . 10. S 11. CX **. . .** gets sick during a flight, the . . . 12. S

Activity 8, p. 131 Answers will vary.

Activity 9, pp. 134–135 1. an 2. The 3. the 4. the 5. a 6. the 7. a 8. a 9. an 10. a 11. the

Activity 10, pp. 135–136 2. Laura's parents visited the Eiffel Tower in Paris last year. 3. Are we going to have a grammar test next week? 4. The weather was very nice for a picnic last Saturday. 5. Carol and Bob saw an owl in a tree in their back yard last night. 6. Do you go to the movies every Friday night? 7. The computer doesn't work anymore. 8. I brought an apple and a sandwich for lunch yesterday. 9. After Nicholas graduated last week, his sister gave him an expensive gift. 10. My dad bought me a bike for my last birthday, but I wanted a puppy.

Activity 11, p. 137 3. S Because it was raining, we didn't go to the beach. 4. F 5. S She arrived late because her car broke down. 6. F 7. S Because I live in New York, I go to the theater on Broadway often. 8. F 9. S The computers were down today because a storm knocked out power. 10. S We are going to postpone the meeting because the managers are going to a conference.

Activity 12, pp. 138–139 Answers will vary.

Activity 13, pp. 139–140 2. Michael likes to play soccer, hockey, and football. 3. My friend Rick is tall, strong, and handsome. 4. John, Robert, and Theo want to go to the movies. 5. When I go to the beach tomorrow, I am going to bring sunglasses, a towel, a cold drink, and a book. 6. At the dance, we ate food, danced, and played games. 7. In Moscow, Candice is going to visit the Kremlin, St. Basil's Cathedral, and Gorky Park. 8. Ron, Harry, and Elizabeth rode the Ferris wheel at the fair.

Activity 14, p. 141

My winter vacation is going to be wonderful because I am going to go to **M**ontreal with my best friend. We *are* going to spend two weeks there, and it is going to be a wonderful time. I have **an** aunt who lives there, and she *is* going to show us all the **beautiful sights**. I don't speak **F**rench very well, so I'm a little bit nervous. After I arrive in Canada, I am going to buy a lot of souvenirs for my parents, brother, and friends.

Activity 15, p. 142 Answers will vary.

UNIT 7

Activity 1, pp. 147–148 1. which/that 2. which 3. who/that 4. who/that 5. who 6. who/that 7. which/that 8. who/that 9. who/that 10. which/that 11. which/that 12. who/that 13. which/that

Activity 2, pp. 148–149 2. New Hampshire is a small state which/that is in the northeastern part of the United States. 3. Romansch is a language which/that comes from Latin. 4. Bolivia is a country in South America which/that does not have a coastline. 5. Nasi lemak is a Malaysian dish which/that uses white rice and coconut milk. 6. Danti Alighieri was an Italian writer who/that wrote *The Divine Comedy*. 7. A meerkat is a rodent which/that is a native of Africa. 8. The *Titanic* was a ship which/that sank in the North Atlantic Ocean. 9. A coach is a person who/that trains athletes to perform well in sports. 10. El Prado is a famous museum, which/that is in the heart of Madrid, Spain.

Activity 3, p. 150 2. The movie that/which we saw on television last night was *Steel Magnolias*. 3. The day that/which we arrived in Texas was October 11. 4. The number that/which Paul gave me was incorrect. 5. The story that/which Samir told was extremely interesting. 6. The homework assignment that/which the grammar teacher gave us was difficult. 7. The man who/that is standing on the street corner is my friend. 8. The food that/which we bought for dinner got cold. 9. The police officer who/that gave me a speeding ticket was very angry. 10. The play that/which we are going to see tonight is very popular in London.

Activity 4, p. 151 1. The teachers <u>who work in the city's schools</u> say they might go on strike. 2. The teachers want to go on strike because they get salaries <u>that are very low</u>. 3. The teachers hope the people <u>who attend the meeting</u> will agree with them about the low salaries.

Activity 5, p. 151 1. The teachers who work in the city's schools say they might go on strike. The teachers say they might go on strike. The teachers work in the city's schools. 2. The teachers want to go on strike because they get salaries that are very low. The teachers want to go on strike. The teachers' salaries are very low. 3. The teachers hope the people who attend the meeting will agree with them about the low salaries. People will attend the meeting. The teachers hope the people will agree with them about the low salaries.

Activity 6, pp. 152–153

Paragraph 57: This is the weather that/which I like the most.

Paragraph 58: Another word that/which causes spelling problems is *its*.

Activity 7, p. 153 a. 1 Sudan is a country that is in the northeastern part of Africa. b. 2 It is a large country with many different people. c. 6 In conclusion, different areas of this country have very different histories. d. 3 The people who live in the southern part of the country were independent for many years. e. 4 However, the people who live in the northern part of the country were under foreign control for long periods of time. f. 5 Some of the countries that ruled this northern area were Egypt, Rome, Turkey, and Britain.

Activity 8, p. 154

Titles may vary.

[Sudan, a Country of Different Histories]

Sudan is a country that is in the northeastern part of Africa. It is a large country with many different people. The people who live in the southern part of the country were independent for many years. However, the people who live in the northern part of the country were under foreign control for long periods of time. Some of the countries that ruled this northern area were Egypt, Rome, Turkey, and Britain. In conclusion, different areas of this country have very different histories.

Activity 9, pp. 155–156 2. Last week the Johnson sisters had an excellent party. (OR The Johnson sisters had an excellent party last week.) 3. Next Monday we are going to buy a new car. (OR We are going to buy a new car next Monday.) 4. Janie exercises at the gym every morning. (OR Every morning Janie exercises at the gym.) 5. Did you take the grammar test yesterday morning in Mrs. Smith's class? (OR Did you take the grammar test in Mrs. Smith's class yesterday morning?) 6. I left my books in my car last night. (OR Last night I left my books in my car.) 7. Two days ago they met Luis at a restaurant. (OR They met Luis at a restaurant two days ago.) 8. Sara is putting the pie in the oven right now. (OR Right now Sara is putting the pie in the oven.) 9. Our friends are going to arrive at the airport in ten minutes. (OR In ten minutes our friends are going to arrive at the airport.) 10. Every day squirrels bury nuts under our oak tree. (Squirrels bury nuts under our oak tree every day.)

Activity 10, pp. 156–157: 1. In two days, Daniel is going to attend an important company meeting in Istanbul, Turkey. 2. His flight is going to leave at 5 P.M. from Gate 32. 3. Daniel is going to put his suitcase in the car in ten minutes.

Activity 11, pp. 157–158 3. S 4. F 5. F 6. S 7. S 8. F 9. F 10. S

Activity 12, p. 158

*There are m*any reasons to visit a new country. First, you can see beautiful**,** interesting**,** and distant places. For example, you can visit *the* Kremlin and Red Square in **M**oscow. Another reason to travel is to eat new types of food. If you visit Thailand, you can drink jasmine tea, *and* you can *eat* coconut-flavored rice. Finally, you can meet new people *who/that* live in these exotic countries. **Y**ou can talk to people and learn more about *their* likes and dislikes. As you can see, traveling to another country is important for *different reasons*.

Activity 13, pp. 158–160 Answers will vary.

UNIT 8

Practice 1, pp. 163–164 A. a. 5 In fact, the Andes affect almost every aspect of Peruvian life. b. 2 It is located in the south-central part of the continent. c. 1 Peru is a country in South America. d. 3 The Andes Mountains run through the middle of the country. e. 4 The mountains affect weather, agriculture, and transportation. B. a. 2 They are classified as birds, but they cannot fly. b. 3 Instead, they are excellent swimmers because they have wings shaped like flippers. c. 5 They live only in the cold regions in the southern hemisphere. d. 1 Penguins are very interesting animals. e. 4 Many people think that these birds live at the North Pole, but they do not.

Practice 2, pp. 164–165 1. fruit 2. believe 3. vegetable because 4. other 5. tomatoes 6. tomatoes 7. really a

Practice 3, p. 165

Last Saturday my father and I built a koi pond in our backyard. First, we dug a big hole in the center of the yard. Then we laid a sheet of black plastic in the hole. Next, we put rocks around the edge of the hole. After that, we filled the new pond with water. Finally, we added plants and fish. It was a lot of hard work, but we enjoyed it.

Practice 4, p. 166

Tomorrow Antonio will plant his first garden. First, he will choose the location of the garden. He will put it in a place that gets a lot of sunlight. Then he will dig up the ground. After that, he will add fertilizer. Next, he will take seeds and plant them in rows in the garden. Finally, he will water the new garden. It will be hard work, but he will be proud of his garden.

Practice 5, p. 167 1. believe 2. used 3. allows 4. helps 5. ended 6. watch 7. listen

1. I believe that the light bulb is one of the most important inventions in the world. 2. eleven 3. (a) Candle light is very weak and difficult to see with, so most work ended at sundown. (b) Without the light bulb, people would not have as many choices for work or play. (c) Now people can work longer hours indoors or outdoors. (d) People can do more fun things after it is dark now. 4. Simple Present—fact, Simple Past—situations that began and ended in the past

Practice 6, p. 168 Answers will vary.

Practice 7, pp. 168–169 1. is going to be 2. get 3. am going to get 4. am going to go 5. start 6. am going to start 7. have 8. am going to go 9. are going to have

1. Tomorrow is going to be a busy day for me. 2. ten 3. (a) He is getting up earlier than usual to go to the gym. (b) He is going to work earlier than usual. (c) He is going to his mom's house instead of eating dinner with friends. (d) They are going to have a big party for his mom. 4. Present Progressive representing the Future tense—planning for the future, Simple Present—indicating routine and use of adverbs of frequency

Practice 8, p. 169 Answers will vary.

Practice 9, p. 170

Paragraph 65: 1. a 2. the 3. the 4. a 5. the 6. the 7. a 8. the 9. The 10. the 11. the

Practice 10, pp. 170–171 Answers will vary.

Practice 11, pp. 171–172 1. My Mustang was bright blue and very powerful. 2. They wanted to drive it, but I told them they could not. 3. My friends didn't want to walk, so they always chose to be passengers. 4. Every weekend I drove to the movie theater in that car, and my friends rode with me.

Practice 12, pp. 172–173 Answers will vary.

Practice 13, p. 173 1. that 2. who 3. that 4. that 5. that 6. that 7. that

Practice 14, p. 174 Answers will vary.

Practice 15, pp. 174–175 1. S T 2. S T 3. T S 4. S T 5. S T

Practice 16, pp. 175–176 a. 6 b. 3 c. 1 d. 5 e. 4 f. 2 g. 7

Practice 17, p. 176 Answers will vary.

Practice 18, pp. 176–177 1. c 2. a 3. c 4. b 5. b

Practice 19, pp. 178–180

Opinion 1

   1. Because second-hand smoke causes cancer, I believe that banning smoking in restaurants and bars is correct. 2. Answers will vary. 3. Smoking is not allowed in building such as post offices and banks. Smoking will one day be against the law.

Opinion 2

   1. I think it's unfair to single out smokers and make them feel unaccepted. 2. Answers will vary. 3. People in bars and restaurants can drink too much and get into fatal accidents.

Opinion 3

   1. I really have mixed feelings about this new law. 2. Answers will vary. 3. She can see both sides of the issue.

Practice 20, pp. 180–181 Answers will vary.

Practice 21, p. 181 Answers will vary.

Practice 22, pp. 181–183

Opinion 1

   1. A court must not have more power over someone's children than the family. 2. Answers will vary. 3. The parents didn't want the operation because of their religion.

Opinion 2

   1. When a human life is involved, the court must have some power in making the decision. 2. Answers will vary. 3. The court only wanted to save a life.

Practice 23, pp. 183–184 Answers will vary.

Practice 24, p. 184 Answers will vary.

APPENDIX 14

Writing Activity 1, pp. 208–209

Florida

   1. Florida is a large state. 2. It is located in the southeastern part of the United States. 3. The population of Florida is approximately 15 million. 4. The largest cities in Florida are Miami, Tampa, and Orlando. 5. Millions of tourists visit this state every year. 6. They come for the beaches, the parks, and the great weather.

Writing Activity 2, p. 209

My Older Brother

1. I'd like to tell you about my older brother. 2. His name is _____ (any boy's name). 3. He is 26 years old. 4. He is an elementary school teacher. 5. He loves children. 6. He is very patient and kind. 7. My brother (any boy's name) is a great person.

Writing Activity 3, p. 210

My House

1. I live in a little house. 2. It is located on Hillside Road. 3. My house number is 7. 4. My house is very old. 5. It is (any number that is old for a house. How about 50?) years old. 6. The sides of my house are white. 7. The roof is dark gray. 8. In front of the house, there are some small bushes and trees. 9. I am so lucky to live in this house!

Writing Activity 4, pp. 210–211

An Ocean Plant

1. Seaweed is an interesting plant. 2. It grows in the ocean. 3. It does not like very hot temperatures. 4. It needs a lot of water to live. 5. Its leaves are long and thin. 6. Many people grow this plant in their aquariums.

Writing Activity 5, pp. 211–212 1. They 2. She 3. It 4. He 5. It 6. They 7. They

Writing Activity 6, pp. 212–213

Possible title: Moving Is Work

1. Last week Jane and I moved into a new apartment. 2. We were very excited. 3. We moved many big things into it. 4. I had a television. 5. We put it in the living room next to the window. 6. Jane's brother helped us move our couch and chairs. 7. We told him to put them in front of the television. 8. Finally, we moved in our beds. 9. It didn't take a long time to bring them in. 10. Jane said she would move her bed by herself, but her brother had to help her. 11. Moving is a lot of hard work. I hope we don't have to move again soon!

Writing Activity 7, pp. 213–214 1. My grandpa is a very busy farmer. 2. Yesterday he got up at four o'clock in the morning. 3. He ate breakfast. 4. Then he went out to the barn. 5. There he fed and milked the cows. 6. When he finished, he fed the rest of the animals. 7. Then he worked in the cornfields until noon. 8. He ate a fast lunch. 9. After that, he worked in the fields again. 10. In the evening, he ate dinner. 11. Then he fed the animals one last time. 12. Grandpa finally went to bed at around nine o'clock. 13. He certainly did a lot in one day!

Writing Activity 8, p. 214 1. He has to go to school every day, and he takes several classes every day. 2. He helps with everyday work there, but he cannot help with emergencies. 3. Lars's grades are very good, so he will graduate with honors.

Writing Activity 9, p. 215 1. When I graduate from high school this year, my aunt and uncle are going to take me on a wonderful vacation. 2. We are going to go to the Black Hills in South Dakota. 3. We are going to do lots of interesting things. 4. We are going to visit Mt. Rushmore and take lots of pictures. 5. We are going to visit a place to mine for gold. 6. One night we are even going to eat buffalo burgers for dinner. 7. It is going to be very exciting. 8. I am going to make memories on that trip that I am going to keep for a lifetime.

Writing Activity 10, pp. 215–216 2. In order to explore the wreck, they used a submersible that was controlled by people on the surface. 3. They even brought things to the surface that were on the sunken ship.